WITHDRAWN

UNDERSTANDING

Contemporary American Drama

BY WILLIAM HERMAN

UNIVERSITY OF SOUTH CAROLINA PRESS

The author gratefully acknowledges that the quotation from Langston Hughes's poem "Note on Commercial Theater" in chapter 5 is
reprinted by permission of Harold Ober Associates Incorporated.
Copyright © 1959 by Langston Hughes.

Published in Columbia, South Carolina, by the
University of South Carolina Press

Manufactured in the United States of America

Library of Congress Cataloging-in-Publication Data

Herman, William, 1926–
  Understanding contemporary American drama.

  (Understanding contemporary American literature)
  Bibliography: p.
  Includes index.
  1. American drama—20th century—History and
criticism. I. Title. II. Series.
PS352.H47   1987   812'.5'09   86-32626
ISBN 0-87249-492-6
ISBN 0-87249-493-4 (pbk.)

For my Uncle Bud Rovit,
who taught me all I know about theater and drama—for which I forgive him.

CONTENTS

EDITOR'S PREFACE

Understanding Contemporary American Literature has been planned as a series of guides or companions for students as well as good nonacademic readers. The editor and publisher perceive a need for these volumes because much of the influential contemporary literature makes special demands. Uninitiated readers encounter difficulty in approaching works that depart from the traditional forms and techniques of prose and poetry. Literature relies on conventions, but the conventions keep evolving; new writers form their own conventions—which in time may become familiar. Put simply, *UCAL* provides instruction in how to read certain contemporary writers—identifying and explicating their material, themes, use of language, point of view, structures, symbolism, and responses to experience.

The word *understanding* in the series title was deliberately chosen. Many willing readers lack an adequate understanding of how contemporary literature works; that is, what the author is attempting to express and the means by which it is conveyed. Although the criticism and analysis in the series have been aimed at a level of general accessibility, these introductory volumes are meant to be applied in conjunction with the works they cover. Thus they do not provide a substitute for the works and authors they introduce, but rather prepare the reader for more profitable literary experiences.

M. J. B.

PREFACE

The purpose of this volume is to introduce the reader to five important contemporary American dramatists and thus enhance understanding of the drama of this period. It also aims to give the background and foreground of their work by surveying the main currents of theater and drama in the period and by looking very briefly at the work of six other playwrights. I begin with 1964—the year that saw Sam Shepard's first plays produced and the year also of the important play *Dutchman*, by Amiri Baraka—and end in 1984, the year of David Rabe's *Hurlyburly*, a work which seems to me to signal a certain dramatic concentration on post–Vietnam consciousness.

Doubtless many will quarrel with my choice of playwrights to examine in detail: a good case could be made for the inclusion of, say, Amiri Baraka or Edward Albee or Arthur Kopit or Adrienne Kennedy; in fact, I could make that case myself. But I could not give extended treatment to all those I would have wished to. Baraka has hardly been heard from in the 80s. Albee seems to be of an earlier generation and his drama to voice that generation's concerns. I could not find in Arthur Kopit's work a unified dramatic vision, though some of his plays are among our most powerful. Adrienne Kennedy seems to have been discour-

PREFACE

aged from continuing to work. So I have selected those writers whose work depends mainly on language rather than theatrical imagery, omitting such important figures as Judith Malina and Julian Beck, Joseph Chaikin, Richard Schechner, Lee Breuer, Charles Ludlum, Richard Foreman, and Robert Wilson, none of whose work is precisely amenable to analysis with reference to a text; I have chosen instead to concentrate on writers who have more or less performed steadily and been performed steadily from the time they made their debuts until near the end date of this study.

To have made such choices is to confer value on their work. So be it. Other critics will doubtless weigh in with other values, and from the whole critical enterprise standards will emerge. The conversation about art has always pursued such choices and emerged with values. In the end the reader may quarrel with my emphases but will not be led astray by my selections.

I wish to thank the following for special contributions to this work: Lanford Wilson and Marsha Norman generously allowed me to work from their manuscripts. Curt Dempster of the Ensemble Studio Theater shared with me his special professional knowledge of David Mamet, Marsha Norman and others, and supplied me with texts otherwise unobtainable. The dancer/actor Daniel Nagrin of the

PREFACE

Department of Dance of the University of Arizona at Tempe permitted me access to materials pertaining to his collaboration with Sam Shepard on their *Jacaranda*. Patricia Galloway of the William Morris Agency supplied me with the Marsha Norman manuscripts. Professor James V. Hatch of the Hatch-Billops Collection in New York generously supplied me with materials on Ed Bullins. Professors Arthur Zeiger and James Greene read parts of the manuscript and made scrupulous suggestions. Professor Edward Quinn was shrewd in advancing ideas, generous in offering encouragement. Professor Saul N. Brody introduced me to the magic of the word processor and thus saved me from extraordinary drudgery. My daughter Donna Ann Herman lent me her considerable and now out-of-print library of Sam Shepard texts. My wife, Joanna, read the manuscript with style and acumen, and to her I owe more than a few of the good ideas to be found in these pages. I thank them all.

UNDERSTANDING

CONTEMPORARY
AMERICAN DRAMA

CHAPTER ONE

Theater and Drama in America: 1964–1984

The Background

America, both in the spectacle of fleshing out the continent and in the drama of incarnating itself as idea, has been the essence of theater. Yet ordinary playgoing began here as an entertainment for country bumpkins emulating their betters in London. Before the twentieth century, in matters theatrical, we were a nation of idolators. With the advent of David Belasco and Eugene O'Neill we began to establish a theatrical tradition of our own. Still, until recently that tradition has been shy of radically modern influences.[1]

Until the end of the 1950s and the beginning of the 60s American theater meant production on Broadway in New York City, frontal staging in a building designed exclusively for theatrical performance, with the curtain representing the fourth wall establishing an illusion of reality. The audience was carefully separated from the players, and the dramas performed were species of light comedy, musicals (an indigenous form that must, unfortunately, be bypassed here entirely), and serious plays that dealt in social criticism—on the order of "war is a horror" and "the family is destructive"—or psychological exploration. Though our theater had produced important dramatists like Eugene O'Neil and, later, Tennessee Williams, Arthur Miller, and Edward Albee, we might just as well have been still importing our plays from London. In 1954 Robert Brustein, Dean of the Yale Drama School, put it that "American drama often seems to be the most mundane form of legitimate culture since eighteenth century sentimental comedy, a form to which it has more than a little resemblance. Our serious drama is informed by a debased Freudianism and our comedies are set in motion by man-chasing women."[2] Indeed, the moribund Broadway of today counts on importing such work to sustain its compromised vitality.

Post–World War II America could not sustain such a mild-mannered enterprise. The great events and the radical intellectual and cultural currents of the 50s and 60s combined to change things in our theater. The changes were reflected by theatrical activity. Off Broadway, which had begun in New York in 1915 with the anticommercial revolt of the Washington Square Players in New York and of the Provincetown Theater on Cape Cod, began to blossom with new companies, new talents in acting and directing and playwriting, and new ideas. The Circle in the Square began to come together as early as 1950. The Living Theater opened its doors in a loft on Upper Broadway in 1951, and the Phoenix Theatre, which lasted long enough into the 60s to present Kopit's *Oh Dad Poor Dad Mama's Hung You in the Closet and I'm Feeling So Sad*, began to operate in 1953. The Circle in the Square gave legitimacy to the whole enterprise with its production of Williams' *Summer and Smoke* (1952), starring Geraldine Page and directed by José Quintero. The power and professionalism of that production attracted an attentive audience and turned a profit. When Carmen Capalbo's production of Brecht's *Three Penny Opera*, with Kurt Weill's widow, Lotte Lenya, in the leading role, began a long run at the Theater des Lys in 1954, the weight and gravity of theater Off Broadway was established beyond doubt. Off Broadway, in fact, became a thriving enterprise.

In 1953 Joseph Papp began his New York Shakespeare Festival, an enterprise that by 1970 employed more actors than any other theatrical enterprise in the United States. Papp moved from free Shakespeare in Central Park to the presentation of radical new works (as well as some conventional ones) and the introduction of such new playwrights as Charles Gordone, David Rabe, Ed Bullins, and David Mamet.

Meanwhile theater across the country was growing and changing. Instead of a few cities with "Little Theaters" and most cities just road stops for touring Broadway attractions, regional theater expanded at a great pace. Seattle and Houston and Washington, for example, were establishing theaters like the Alley Theater in Houston, the Arena Stage in Washington, and the Seattle Repertory Company. These theaters, later joined by the Hartford Stage Company, the Mark Taper Forum in Los Angeles, and the Playhouse in Cincinnati, performed the classics mainly but were also in the thick of encouraging new writers and trying out new methods of acting and staging.

Within a few years ferment and revolt attended this burgeoning; with the establishment of Joe Cino's Caffe Cino in 1958 and the Cafe La Mama of Ellen Stewart in 1960, the new venue of Off Off Broadway was born. And the avant-garde theater began to take shape. Caffe Cino, a coffee house, introduced the work of Lanford Wilson. La Mama, another, gave playing space to such writers as Wilson, Paul Foster, Jean-Claude Van Itallie, Sam Shepard, and Ross Alexander. Theaters sprang up in churches. The Judson Poets' Theater

THEATER AND DRAMA IN AMERICA

established the careers of Maria Irene Fornes and Ronald Tavel. Theater Genesis, which produced Sam Shepard's first plays, was in the basement of the ancient St. Mark's-in-the-Bowerie.

By 1963 Joseph Chaikin's Open Theater was giving performances in Sheridan Square, and the Free Southern Theater of John O'Neal and Gilbert Moses was presenting *Waiting for Godot* to black audiences in the Mississippi Delta. The Guthrie in Minneapolis, the American Conservatory Theater in San Francisco, and the Seattle Repertory Company all started up in 1963, and the American Place Theatre of New York began in St. Clement's Church in 1964.

In retrospect a miraculous year, 1964 was the year of Amiri Baraka's powerful and influential American play *Dutchman*, as well as the first plays of Sam Shepard. In the same year Susan Sontag published her important essay "Against Interpretation," which spoke out against interposing meaning between an auditor and the direct experience of art. That same year the Actor's Theater of Louisville, which was to bring Marsha Norman to the fore in the late 70s and early 80s, took its first steps. The trauma of Vietnam inaugurated a decade-long theatrical response in the form of street and guerrilla theater. The urgencies of the civil rights movement motivated black theater across

UNDERSTANDING CONTEMPORARY DRAMA

the country from Los Angeles and San Francisco to the Negro Ensemble Company and the New Lafayette Theater in New York. El Teatro Campesino arose in 1965 to support a strike of migrant workers in California. By the end of the 60s gay theater was alive at the Ridiculous Theatrical Company in New York. Richard Schechner, up from New Orleans and the *Tulane Drama Review*, created the Performance Group on Wooster Street in New York, and a few blocks away the Circle Repertory Company and Woodie King, Jr.'s New Federal Theater were in full swing.

The 70s saw the full emergence of the avant-garde tendencies in American theater with the work of Robert Wilson, Richard Forman, and Lee Breuer. Their work, described as the Theater of Images by Bonnie Marranca, used painting and sculpture within a proscenium arch to offer the viewer an experience of meditative dream (Wilson), broke up the continuity of consciousness into the bits and pieces of imagining (Foreman), and concentrated on images of essential being (Breuer). New enterprises continued to spring up. Curt Dempster began his Ensemble Studio Theater in New York and inaugurated an ongoing workshop for new theater talent. The Goodman Theatre in Chicago lit up with new energy. Black theater emerged in the New Lafayette and elsewhere. But

THEATER AND DRAMA IN AMERICA

by the mid-70s responding perhaps to a changed mood in America—the economic crunch initiated by the Arab oil embargo of 1973, a post–Watergate, post–Vietnam quiet and conservatism—an impulse of fifteen years had begun to lose its force. The Open Theater had closed and the Living Theater began to break up into splinter groups. From an emphasis on public, political, and ritual art there began to grow an emphasis on performance ensembles—communities of actors plying their trade without heed of politics—and the intensely private art of visions: Wilson, Foreman, and Breuer. Though these artists were programmatically avant-garde, and though many of our important playwrights were working productively, the sense of a fomenting experimentalism diminished.

Although aesthetic reasons have been advanced for this falling off, the problem was identified by Bigsby as social. "The theatre," he said, was "no longer felt to be at the centre of cultural life as for a time it had seemed to be."[3] Paradoxically, this analysis might be more accurately applied to cultural life in the early 60s—when theater was booming. The theatrical diminution of the mid-70s, which carried over to the early 80s, seems rather the result of a profound shift in cultural and technological habit—the new cross-generational allegiances to electronics, to recorded music, film, television and its ancillaries, cable and the VCR. Yet our most vibrant theater still goes on, touched to its core by issues very like the following.

The Foreground

The plays and performances of the period exhibited enormous variety and distinction, and it is impossible to take account of everything that went on. Nevertheless, some things are clear. Outside of Broadway the expansive and radical theatrical activity of the period up to the mid-70s was characterized by the adoption of aesthetic theory and practice, and by social attitudes and allegiances, that were directly at odds with the prevailing aesthetics of American theater and the prevailing social and cultural ideas in force.

Intellectual and Social Currents

The interplay of ideas and social life helped shape American theater of the period. For example, the sensibilities of American artists in the post–World War II period were ripe for opportunities to reject the rational, liberal, democratic structures that had governed our national life and culture. The advent of total destructive capability;

THEATER AND DRAMA IN AMERICA

the exposure of the structure and personalities of our governance as fragile at best and corrupt at worst; the wars in Korea and Vietnam (the Tet offensive of 1968 and the demonstrations at the Pentagon, in particular); the Chicago Seven; civil rights; the assassinations of the Kennedys, the Mississippi Headstart workers, and Martin Luther King, Jr.; the tremendous pressures of minorities to assert their agendas—all these led to and in some respects ratified the counterculture of the 60s and its ideation. That ideation mistrusted language that had been debased by corrupt politics, sought solace and salvation in mysticism and Eastern philosophies, and in art looked for a set of avant-garde practices that would end in sexual, political, and artistic liberation. The mood was summed up by Richard Schechner of the Performance Group, who noted in 1968: "In a world where law fails . . . lawlessness and chaotic sensuality are attractive."[4] We may refer Schechner's "law" that failed not only to government but to artistic practices as well.

Among the young the historical moment engendered *authenticity* as the key concept of the personal and the public life. To live the "authentic" life, behavior and action needed to be brought in line with felt experience, unmediated by old American liberal, progressive tendencies. This program was set in a matrix of emerging and influential notions about sexual liberation, an event that, it was thought, might lead to political liberation. The disseminators of these ideas included Wilhelm Reich, who influenced two generations with *The Function of the Orgasm* (1942) and *Character Analysis* (1945). Reich's notion was that orgasmic sexuality was a measure of total health and would inevitably lead to political change, since healthy individuals make healthy political institutions. Norman O. Brown in *Life Against Death* (1959) and *Love's Body* (1968) emphasized the inherent sexuality of the social life and the need to heal the schism between mind and body, a notion also present in Herbert Marcuse's *Eros and Civilization* (1955). The interest in Eastern religions, principally the Zen Buddhism explained in the work of Alan Watts, centered on the advocacy of a relaxed acceptance of being and experience; what would happen would happen, and thus the idea of chance as an element of experience was given status.

These ideas were embodied in various degrees in the performance theaters. The Living Theatre was concerned with "the authenticity of the body."[5] Its productions began to emphasize the meditative, and the company performed works like *The Marrying Maiden* of Jackson Maclow, which had been inspired by the avant-garde musician/

THEATER AND DRAMA IN AMERICA

artist John Cage, and which depended on the *I Ching: The Book of Changes*. The agenda of their work included, in fact, a rebellion against "social structures in the name of spontaneous feeling."[6] *Mysteries and Smaller Pieces* (1964),* their first communal creation—improvised by the company without benefit of a writer with a text—made physical contact between audience and players. Julian Beck suggested that its technique was subversive, the players having the "courage not to be cast in a role,"[7] but rather being themselves and blurring the distinction between life and art. Politically such work had more value than a mere play. It was a "secret weapon of the people."[8] The height of this practice was reached with *Paradise Now* (1968). It was to use the mysterious forces of Zen, Kabbalah, ritual, color, randomness, and noise to "demystify the state"—to change utterly its audience. Beck observed, with a passionate naïveté hard to credit in 1987, that it would be impossible to do this play and "not free anyone [in the audience] who might not be free."[9]

The acting exercises of Joseph Chaikin's Open Theater started with "the body in motion,"[10] for the central focus of its productions was on sound

---

* Dates following plays are dates of first performance or first performance in New York, whichever is later.

and movement, actors chanting and moving together in physical and aural concert. "All of one's past—historically and evolutionary," he noted, "is contained in the body."[11] Unlike the Living Theater's later practice of creation without texts, the Open Theater relied on such writers as Megan Terry and Jean-Claude Van Itallie to supply, along with the director, a central intelligence. Chaikin created an extraordinary ensemble company that celebrated the presence of the actor and discovered ways of uniting mind with body through the actor's realization of a transforming text.

Richard Schechner's Performance Group, committed to an organicism that used the rituals of preliterate societies as a dramatic score, also sought the liberation of the body and the consequent breakdown of the line between art and life, actor and role. *Dionysus in 69* was performed in a converted garage in which the group built a rough wooden "environment" intended to rearrange the audience's relation to the players. Actors were introduced individually and the audience let in the same way, one at a time, with Schechner acting the impressario at the door. The escape into the streets at the end was a calculated gesture aimed at, once again, linking art and life, politics and theater.

THEATER AND DRAMA IN AMERICA

Aesthetic Ideas

Rejecting the form and practice of Broadway theater, the radical theater favored the communal style of ensemble work, forgoing a new political aesthetic of theater work, emulating the Berliner Ensemble, the Group Theatre and the Moscow Art. Theater sought not just to provide aesthetic experience of a particular kind but to change the world and redefine the relations between audience and players.

In the modern theater since Richard Wagner, the other arts have never been entirely "other." Theater has always been an amalgam of all the arts. Still, the other arts have made specific contributions to our contemporary theater.

An important one came from the crossover of painters and sculptors into the theater in the late 50s and early 60s. The term *happening*, coined by Allen Kaprow in 1959, marked the theatricalization of artistic ideas derived from surrealism and dada. Kaprow, Robert Whitman, Jim Dine, and Claus Oldenburg staged events like Oldenburg's *Moviehouse* and Kaprow's *The Courtyard*. In happenings environments were created, at first in art galleries, but later in other odd spaces through which an audience moved, played, or was directed in tasks, becoming part of the artwork and participating in easing the separation between spectator and event, life and art. Frequently made up of objects found in everyday life, happenings had no metaphorical meaning. Mattresses, a suitcase full of lemons, crude cloth curtains, cubicles with silent movies running in each, combs "played" for their "music"—all these were the detritus of ordinary experience given new value through mere presence and an audience's concentration on them. The experience of the physical world was all, and a heightened consciousness was the expected result. And in elevating these objects to such heights, happenings contributed to erasing the distinction between high and low art—an important development in modern art that shows up in any number of plays. When, in Shepard's *La Turista* (1967), Kent leaps through the back wall, leaving his outline there and ending the play, a pure happening has taken place.

It is harder to trace the entry of forms like rock music, film, and video into the theater, yet these things are part of the new aesthetic. The central role of rock in Shepard's plays, the cinematic form of a play like Kopit's *Indians* (1968), and dozens of plays with screened projections testify to the incorporation of these elements.

The physical and commercial occasion of new theater frequently governed the form of theatrical presentation. The short (one-act) form tended to be the dominant one because it was most suitable for the available space and the occasion. Lanford Wilson's *Balm in Gilead* (1965) was the first full-length original play presented Off Off Broadway. But he and others were adept at the one-, two-, and three-character one-act play that could work on a one-foot platform set against a blank wall in a cramped space. His *Madness of Lady Bright* (1966), a one-character (and two shade) psychological study, is an example of a work whose form was dictated by the presentation space. Israel Horovitz's *The Indian Wants the Bronx* (1967), with three characters and a telephone booth, is another. Moreover, these spaces generated excitement just because they had what Peter Brook called "roughness." "A haphazard hall," he went on, "may be a tremendous meeting place: this is the mystery of the theatre."[12] Excitement was generated by the juxtaposition of the rough space of, say, Caffe Cino and the full-length productions given there of *Antigone* and *The Importance of Being Earnest*.

The audience in the players' laps looked forward to and enhanced an important aesthetic idea that would move performance companies like the Living Theater and the Performance Group; namely, that the separation of audience and players was a false and arbitrary one and inconsistent with an ideal of breaking down the barriers between theater and spectator. Of course, the one-act play was also a complex issue of both tradition and revolt; O'Neil in America and any number of Europeans had worked in the form, and American writers of the period were following them. Moreover, a short play of indeterminate length was a piece of aesthetic rebellion against the straitjacket of traditional form and length.

The theorists Antonin Artaud, through the translation of his influential book *The Theatre and Its Double* (1958), and Jerzy Grotowski, through his visit to America in 1967 and his book *Towards a Poor Theatre* (1968), helped shape American theater. Artaud's was a vision of theater as transformational magic. Theater would awake the mysteries and ecstasies. It would react against language and psychology and plot in favor of disturbing imagery and gesture. It would uncover truth away from traditional theater buildings in a mystical space. Seeing lacerating images of cruelty on stage, Artaud suggested, would make it impossible for an audience to *be* cruel outside the theater. Artaud was eagerly assimilated by an American theater waiting for just such a theorist.

Grotowski's "poor" theater was rich in ideas that appealed to the avant-garde. It was a theater that emphasized the actor and his rigorous, almost religiously austere training. Grotowski's theater would be poor only in the accouterments of illusionist theater, for like Artaud, he advocated the revelation of truth through the integrity of performance. Performance for Grotowski was the very subject of theater. The actor "does not tell a story, or create an illusion—he is there in the present."[13] As Joseph Papp commented, on a performance of *Apocalypse* by Grotowski's Polish Laboratory Theatre in 1970, "It is a fully realized work of art, not merely commentary on the world but set into the world."[14]

The most influential practitioner was Beckett. Three times in the period Beckett's *Waiting for Godot* was given significant production. Even Broadway succumbed. Herbert Blau's San Francisco Actors' Workshop took the play to San Quentin prison, where it made a large and immediate impression. The Free Southern Theater took the play into the black communities of the South. It is one of the two plays Sam Shepard has acknowledged as an influence. In fact, it is hard to believe that anybody in contemporary American theater has not taken it into account. As David Mamet has remarked, "Beckett and Pinter—of course I'm influenced by them. If you're in modern dance how could you not be influenced by Martha Graham?"[15]

When Alan Schneider was getting ready to

direct *Waiting for Godot* in New York, he went to Paris to ask Beckett what the play meant. The writer gave the perfect modernist answer: *Godot* had no meaning and no symbolism and no general point of view. "It's just about two people who are like that."[16] For Beckett's play has what Alain Robbe-Grillet in theorizing about fiction calls "presence."[17] Presence, for Robbe-Grillet, is the immediacy of objects and gestures, the simple value of their existence rather than their place in a world of meaning. In this and in other ways Beckett's work is minimalist art. We make what we will of what is there. Things happen from moment to moment, and we react to the physical events on stage. The play has been mercilessly milked for meaning—as if Beckett had not assured us that a different aesthetic applied, as if its distinctive air of uncertainty needed to be ignored—but the essence of its power is its moment-to-moment tragicomedy in a barren cosmic context. The idea of waiting for a salvation that never arrives is now a common-place structural plan used not only by Jack Gelber, but by David Mamet and Sam Shepard as well. The spare, comic language that resonates with effect is already a familiar expression of the modern theatrical idiom. In the play's power to reveal truth through imagistic performance it is Artaudian. In the rigor and minimalism of its gestures it belongs as an underpinning of Grotowski's theory. In its unstable movements it seems to be a happening.

Not all contemporary American theater is avant-garde or experimental. The conventional is still on the boards. But it would be safe to say that in the period under review America joined a grand procession, for the modernist impulse came into the American theater and touched its most talented people. The provincial reflex of reaching in supplication toward a capital city seems to have been expunged. Fragmentation, collage, experiment, the integrated use of other arts, subject matter closer to experience than the liberal imagination permitted—all these can be seen now in American theaters. And the playwrights studied in the following chapters have all been touched in some way by the ideas discussed here. The one to start with is Sam Shepard.

Notes

1. Nearly the whole of this chapter is indebted to C. W. E. Bigsby, *A Critical Introduction to Twentieth-Century American Drama*, vol. 3 (New York: Cambridge University Press, 1985), the exhaustive study of this period. I have also relied on Doris Auerbach, *Sam Shepard, Arthur Kopit and the Off Broadway Theater* (Boston: Twayne, 1982); Stuart Little, *Off Broadway: the Prophetic Theater* (New York: Coward, McCann, 1972); Howard Greenberger, *The Off Broadway Experience* (Englewood

Cliffs, NJ; Prentice-Hall, 1971); Theodore Shank, *American Alternative Theatre* (New York: Oxford University Press, 1982); and Gerald M. Berkowitz, *New Broadways: Theatre Across America 1950–1980* (Totowa, NJ: Littlefield, 1982).

2. Quoted Morris Freedman, *American Drama in Social Context* (Carbondale: Southern Illinois University Press, 1971) 101.

3. Bigsby 35.

4. Richard Schechner, *Public Domain: Essays on the Theatre* (New York: Avon, 1970) 120.

5. Bigsby 81.

6. Bigsby 81.

7. Quoted Bigsby 84.

8. Bigsby 85.

9. Quoted Bigsby 88.

10. Bigsby 98.

11. Quoted Bigsby 98.

12. Peter Brook, *The Empty Space* (New York: Atheneum, 1968) 65.

13. Quoted Bigsby 59.

14. Quoted Little 279.

15. Mel Gussow, "The Daring Visions of Four New, Young Playwrights," *New York Times* 30 Nov. 1977: 13.

16. Alan Schneider, *Entrances: An American Director's Journey* (New York: Viking, 1986) 224.

17. Bigsby 53.

CHAPTER TWO

Geography of a Play Dreamer: *Sam Shepard*

Biography and Approaches to the Work

Samuel Shepard Rogers, known early in his life as Steve Rogers, was born in Fort Sheridan, Illinois, 5 November 1943. His father, the sixth of a line all bearing the name Samuel Shepard Rogers, was an army air corps officer and, his son once added, a Spanish teacher. The family—two daughters, Sam, and the mother, Jane Schook Rogers—moved from airfield to airfield, including one on Guam, before settling down on a farm in Duarte, in rural Southern California, where they tried to make a go of it raising sheep and growing avocados.[1]

In some respects young Shepard was at home in the pickup truck culture of farmland California. He held various odd jobs, including one on a ranch. He became fond of working around livestock—horses and chickens and sheep—showed a champion ram at the Los Angeles County Fair, and thought he might take his father's suggestion and become a veterinarian. In an autobiographical sketch he remembered that at the same fair "I became a thief . . . we used to steal goose eggs and goat's milk for breakfast."[2] He took a shine to his father's drums—the elder Shepard is described by his son as a severe disciplinarian but a lover of jazz and a musician in a band that played local engagements for money—becoming, in his own words, "better" at the drums than his father.[3] He went to jail in a town called Big Bear because he gave the finger to the police chief's wife; he turned over some cars, drank, learned about drugs; he liked to watch cowboy actors riding in the Rose Bowl Parade. He acted in the local community theater and he wrote his first play—now lost.

Though interested in writing—at the time the big influences on him were the beat generation writers, Ferlinghetti and Corso and Kerouac—he enrolled in a junior college to major in education. After three semesters, however, he dropped out. There was also "this big fight with my old man and at that point I fled."[4] Hooking up with a troupe of actors, he toured the country playing in churches, until he landed in New York early in 1963. Shepard's father would become a haunting figure in his work.

In New York the making of an American playwright began with a name change: Steve

SAM SHEPARD

Rogers became Sam Shepard. With a painter friend, Charles Mingus, Jr., he rented an apartment on the Lower East Side. Living was cheap in the area, and from the rest of the country it gathered new arrivals who had come to try to make art. "On the Lower East Side there was a special sort of culture developing. . . . Something was going on . . . People were arriving from Texas and Arkansas and a community was being established. It was a very exciting time."[5] Stimulated by this scene, specifically by a jazz music crowd that he was running with, Shepard's career took off in a burst of feverish playwriting activity—apparently his characteristic way of working (he has noted that writing *Chicago* was a day's work).

While working as a waiter at a Greenwich Village nightclub, he learned that the headwaiter was looking for new plays. This man, Ralph Cook, was about to inaugurate Theater Genesis in the basement of St. Mark's-in-the-Bowerie. He "came up" (presumably to the playwright's apartment) and read his waiter's work, and the result was Shepard's first productions—*Cowboys* and *The Rock Garden*. A couple of months later began his association with Ellen Stewart and the La Mama Experimental Theatre Club, and he was fully launched on a career that has so far produced forty plays,[6] five screenplays, two books of assorted prose and

poetry, and a nonfiction work—an account of Bob
Dylan's national Rolling Thunder tour of 1975.
Along with the impulse to write, the urge has been
strong in Shepard, as in Miss Scoons in *Angel City*,
to become a star: "I am the star." As late as 1971 he
was in England for the express purpose of trying to
realize an old dream—joining a rock and roll
band—for, as he had said, "I don't want to be a
playwright, I want to be a rock and roll star."[7]
Earlier in his career he was a member of a rock
group, the Holy Modal Rounders (in addition to
drums he plays guitar and keyboards), and he has
become lately, in a kind of mythic dream fulfill-
ment, a movie star, with noteworthy talent as an
actor. Since 1975 he has maintained a steady connection with the Magic Theatre of San Francisco—
both as playwright and director of his own work.
He has subsequently worked with the Open Theater of Joseph Chaikin.

These are the outlines of Shepard's life. The
substance of that life is woven through his plays,
forming dramatic images, serving as the ground on
which his imagination does its work. It has many
ingredients: the geography and mythology of the
West—Western deserts; cowboys and Hopi Indians; what he has called "a car culture for the
young" and a "kind of junk magic"[8] that exists in
the small towns of Southern California; the seduc-

SAM SHEPARD

tive power and the tinsel of Hollywood; the heavy metal of rock and roll, not "them sweethearts of the guitar pick ballad school" but what he has called "hard ass shit kickin' music"[9] that informs rock plays like *Cowboy Mouth* and *Angel City*, among others; the contemporary culture that he has absorbed—principally television, comic book, and pop art, the dreck and schlock of his time; bits and pieces of the work of playwrights like Beckett and Brecht and of the mythic realities of romantic poets like Nerval and Rimbaud; a mastery of the mixed media techniques of happenings and the-ater-as-sculpture; a feel for the authenticity of farm and animal life; an acknowledgement of violence on the edge of the American experience; a great taste for restless wandering; and, perhaps most important, an overriding belief in the primacy of spirit and its manifestations in magic and witch-craft.

To begin to approach Shepard, then, we must rid ourselves of ordinary ideas of what consititutes the theatrical experience, either as readers or as playgoers. This is true if we wish to obtain access to the work from *Rock Garden* to *Geography of a Horse Dreamer*. In ordinary theater, for example, actors work at inhabiting roles. The task is to create, say, somebody named Blanche Dubois, an English teacher from Mississippi who is in New Orleans

UNDERSTANDING CONTEMPORARY DRAMA

visiting her sister Stella, married to a roughneck Polish worker named Stanley Kowalski, and who—but by the time this psychosocial tale is fully fleshed out by the actors, the play is over. What the actors do (because the play demands it) is to work at building realistic detail, the sum total of which then becomes meaning inextricably tied to plausibility. Without the plausibility there is no meaning; but, paradoxically, a chief criticism of the well-made realistic play, where plausibility is everything, is that it is not convincing. This is because an excess of plausibility breeds its antibody. So much plausibility becomes implausible.

On the other hand, actors in the early Shepard plays were never directed by the script to engage in building plausibility. On the contrary, the script asked them to forgo tasks that produced "believable" characters. Instead, they were asked to do just what the script told them to do. Shepard was firm about this: "In New York . . . Everybody's [i.e., all the actors are] acting, and doing some lifestyle sort of thing at the same time, sort of mixing their lifestyles with their acting."[10] Instead of actors acting, the doings Shepard devised— visual, bizarre, metaphoric, dramatic, like the tasks of happenings and games of truth and consequences and charades—*affected* the audience.

As Shepard got on in the theater—as he got

SAM SHEPARD

more and more involved with actors and submitted more and more to their ethos—a not-so-subtle change came over his work. Actors, who hate roleless roles—roles that do not permit them to flesh out the lines of the script with stage activities that create plausibility, enabling them to exhibit their lifestyles, so to speak—actors, including Shepard the actor, had their way with him, and he began to produce the plays of his last period, the so-called realistic works. Thus the late plays—from *Curse of the Starving Class* through *Fool for Love*—are filled with what are called "well-rounded" characters. Yet none of these plays is entirely without an interpenetrating theatricality of the early, pristine Shepard.

Examples could be multiplied of the way Shepard's expressive theater does its work. As it does it, moreover, it embodies American themes of vigorous power and mystery: the quarrel with paternal authority, the loss of the land and the fall from an Edenic possibility into an iron city, the transgressions and impingements on the artist by the interests of commercial greed, the recesses of the psyche and the personifications of the beasts in its crevices, the old West and the new. For Shepard, despite the hype and hullabaloo springing up around his movie stardom and his public persona, is a major theatrical artist.

UNDERSTANDING CONTEMPORARY DRAMA

Major Works

The Tooth of Crime (1972)

The play was first produced in London at the Open Space 17 July 1972 under the direction of Charles Marowitz, with original music by Shepard. The first American production was at the McCarter Theatre in Princeton, New Jersey, in November of the same year. The New York premiere was the production by The Performance Group in March, 1973. It is perhaps the most frequently revived of Shepard's works.

All the action is on a determinedly mythic level. The characters are the archetypes Hoss and Crow, amalgams of contending brothers, a son succeeding his father, cowboys in a shootout, rival race-car drivers, rock stars who are one and two on the charts, opposing candidates for public office—or any pair in American life in a savage state of aggressive competition. "Time warps don't shift the purpose," Crow says, "just the style" (231).[11] The world that Hoss and Crow inhabit is made up of a "a bare stage except for an evil-looking black chair . . . something like a Pharaoh's throne" (203), characters in dazzling costumes, musical numbers, and the complex drama of waiting for the showdown, which is act 1, leading up to the showdown itself—act 2. This world is given life by

SAM SHEPARD

the power of Shepard's dialogue, an invented, razor-edged, incantatory argot mainly from the world of rock music but also from other strands of our culture.

Hoss is the champion marker, or killer—when he first appears he is fondling his guns—who is ready to "boogie"; but the Star-Man, the "gazer" he's hired, thinks it's a "pretty risky" time for another kill because Venus is entering Scorpio (205). Hoss is under attack from a number of challengers, much as were the old Western gunfighters—or current boxing champions, mayors, or league leading batters. The challengers are young; one of them, Hoss says, "is just like me only younger" (247), but "I'm gettin' old" (208). He can "smell blood" but he also knows he's "falling behind" (205). Mojo Root Force has "rolled the big one" and knocked over Vegas, Hoss's territory; Vegas was his "mark," and it says so "on my ticket." What Mojo has done is "against the code," a serious but increasingly ordinary offense. Without the code "soloing" would be lost, to be replaced by "gang war," "rumbles," and "honor lost" (206-207). Hoss is besieged and so angry at this particular transgression that he is thinking of joining up with Little Willard to form a gang and annihilate Mojo Root Force. But he is warned against this by his adviser:

UNDERSTANDING CONTEMPORARY DRAMA

You gotta hold steady, Hoss. . . . You don't want to be a fly-by-night mug in the crowd. You want some-thing durable, something lasting. How're you gonna cop an immortal shot if you give up soloing and go into gang war. Sure, you'll have a few moments of global glow, maybe even an interplanetary flash. But it won't last, Hoss (206).

Nevertheless, to get what he wants Hoss de-cides, "Gotta kick scruples. Go against the code" like his heroic models: "That's what they used to do. The big ones. Dylan. Jagger. Townsend" (207). With this assertion the play shades into a dramatic expression of art and artist in America, especially the artist's need to make an ecstatic no-holds-barred leap into the mysterious sources of energy and style. Such leaps go above and beyond rules, games, codes. "Genius is something outside the game. The game can't contain a true genius" (207). Yet, paradoxically, Hoss predicts the next genius wil be a Gypsy Killer, a maverick. Art is made by the unbound. This suggests that leaving the fold (going against the code) and staying in it (playing the game by its rules) are both aspects of a single artistic process. For though genius is outside the game, "without a code, it's just crime. No art involved. No technique, finesse. No sense of mas-tery. The touch is gone" (216). Commercial inter-ests are on the rule-ridden, circumscribed side of this duality. When Hoss argues that he was "born to kill" (206), a natural talent, so to speak, Becky Lou counters with "you gotta listen to management" or wind up a "mad dog"; moreover, without management's capacity to shape the artist's career, the artist self-destructs. "When we first landed you," she says, "you were a complete beast of nature"; then "we molded and shaped you . . . because we saw in you a true genius killer" (207).

But Hoss is still shaky in his resolve and sends for a DJ. With the entrance of Galactic Jack the dramatic environment becomes familiar: the embattled star/hero/leader, shut up in a castle/mansion/fortress, surrounded by his minions, building up the information he needs before making his next move. Hoss revs up his purpose once again and decides on the gang alliance with Little Willard. But despite an impassioned plea to his driver ("We've become respectable and safe. . . . What's happened to our killer heart. What's happened to our blind . . . courage! . . . We were warriors once" 215), Cheyenne insists on "just playin' the game," and it is learned that Willard has been found, a suicide, in, significantly, New Haven, site of Yale, a center of the Eastern establishment, and a place where plays headed for Broadway are "tried out." On top of this a Gypsy Killer is headed toward Hoss, under contract as a hit man to Mojo Root Force.

Hoss gets more and more restless and wants to travel, but it's too dangerous to step out of his place. Instead Becky Lou sings him a song about the magic properties of a soothing highway and the "song that the V-8 sings" (220). He and Becky discuss emotions and the role they will play in the encounter. Hoss fears the loss of his "neutral field state" (222) and tells the story of a high school escapade when courage came with movie images of emotion linked to John Wayne, Robert Mitchum, and Kirk Douglas. As the act nears an end and Hoss's frenzy mounts, he thinks first of extremes of emotion, living on the edge of suicide, and death on the road, with the names of Jimmy Dean, Duane Allman, and Jackson Pollock sung out in a form of sympathetic magic. But the act ends with Hoss talking to himself, evoking his father, slipping into the man's voice and mannerisms to instill courage in himself. His father's final word is, "You're just a man, Hoss" (225).

Act 2 begins with no further introduction. The hit man, Crow, who "looks just like Keith Richard," is on. "He exudes violent arrogance and cruises the stage with true contempt" (227). Shepard had conceived Crow "from a yearning toward violence".

SAM SHEPARD

A totally lethal human with no way or reason for tracing how he got that way. He just appeared. He spit
words that became his weapons. He doesn't "mean"
anything. He's simply following his most savage in-
stincts. He speaks in an upheard-of tongue. He
needed a victim, so I gave him one. He devoured him
just like he was supposed to.[12]

The first words he speaks, "Razor, Leathers. Very
razor" (227), set the tone for the unheard-of
tongue. These words *are* weapons, for Hoss
doesn't get far in understanding Crow: "Can't you
back the language up, man. I'm too old to follow
the flash" (220). Crow's violence toward Hoss
resides not only in language but in his infinite
capacity for imitation; he can mimic Hoss to perfection and does so immediately after act 2 begins.
And Hoss had a premonition about this in act 1:
"His style is copping my patterns. I can feel it and
he's not even here yet" (222). There is nothing
quite so damaging. To mimic another is to displace
him, to crawl into his skin and "wear him like a
suit a' clothes" (247).

Their bout occupies the first part of act 2 and is
overseen by a "Ref" who looks like an NBA referee
with a baseball cap. The contest is a war of words,
with each contender speaking at the other's weakness—wounding with language and raising the
stakes to the ultimate heights for each. Shame and

a sense of smallness are evoked in Hoss by Crow's winning dialogue of round 1; first, Hoss's warm-up routine, in which he plays the old-time cowboy, makes Crow nervously sense that he is losing the match; then the obliterating of Crow's weak sense of being by Hoss's spellbinding recitation of American music's historical roots in the origins of jazz in New Orleans and Chicago. Hoss's best shot is not enough, however; for when the Ref declares that despite Hoss's clear win round 2 is a draw, and that Hoss has lost by a TKO, the champion killer can't take it and guns the Ref down.

The shooting is a sign of his weakness. Hoss capitulates at that point and strikes a deal with Crow. He gives him his turf. "Now show me how to be a man" (243). In the midst of the lesson Hoss is further undone by Becky Lou's performance as a young girl fighting off the unwanted sexual advances of an awkward youth—clearly Hoss, and clearly sapping him of his remaining strength by suggesting the fumbling adolescent weakness of early sexual experience. Moreover, he cannot really do what Crow is suggesting in his teaching: imitate. He tries:

> *HOSS:* Mean and tough and cool. Untouchable. A true killer. Everything's whole and unshakeable (247).

But Hoss is vulnerable, and this recital of knighthood's powerful "neutral field state" ends in Hoss screaming: "IT AIN'T ME! IT AIN'T ME! IT AIN'T ME!" (247). The Four Guys sing an appropriate song: "I saw my face in yours—I took you for myself / I took you by mistake—for me." Crow, however, **can** make himself into others.

CROW: The image is my survival kit.
HOSS: Survival. Yeah. You'll last a long time Crow. A real long time. You're a master adapter. A visionary adapter.
CROW: Switch to suit, Leathers, and mark to kill (249).

When he was on top, in the first act, Hoss could "handle the image like a . . . jockey"; the trouble is, "It's just that I don't trust the race no more. I dropped the blinkers" (208). Now with clear vision Hoss can only commit suicide as Little Willard did, a final piece of a different kind of artistry. It is the artistic end that Hoss envisioned at the end of act 1 when he associated the artistic death with Jimmy Dean, Duane Allman, and Jackson Pollock and looked at the life of a luminescent star as a kind of a fight against the self (224). The stage is cleared of his body and life goes on—uncertainly, with another fragile, vulnerable king at the top of the hill.

UNDERSTANDING CONTEMPORARY DRAMA

Curse of the Starving Class (1976)

EMMA: What kind of a family is this?

Curse was first performed at the Royal Court Theatre in London in June of 1977. The American premiere took place under the auspices of the New York Shakespeare Festival at the Public Theatre, 2 March 1978, directed by Robert Woodruff. It won an Obie award as the best new play of the 1977–1978 season. The play is the first in what Shepard calls his "family trilogy." Each deals with the family as other of his plays have not (though he had begun his career in 1964 with a father, mother and son in *The Rock Garden*)—that is, each focuses on a single family and the particular dynamic by which they live, or fail to live. Moreover, each centers on the family's life on the farm or, as in the case of *True West*, its inauthentic life away from the farm. The farm here is based on the one near Duarte where Shepard lived with his parents and sisters. The farm in *Buried Child* is that of his grandparents. In this group of plays, though family life is a problem at best and savage at worst, the farm is seen as the only authentic place where family life has a chance to thrive. When the farm is neglected and allowed to deteriorate or, worst of all, sold off to developers, the loss is devastating.

Inevitably, moreover, the devastation is linked

to the destruction of the family and the destruction wrought by family life—as if the family could survive, and sponsor the growth and survival of its individual members, only in some Edenic landscape where it could avoid a Fall into the condition of the city. For as Wesley tells his sister, when developers take over, "There'll be bulldozers crashing through the orchard" and "steel girders spanning acres of land" (163). Fecundity will be displaced by something worse than death: "A zombie city!" Wesley cries out. "Right here! Right where we're living now" (163). When the play begins, this despised condition is about to be brought on by both parents; each has made a separate arrangement to sell off the property whose ownership is a matter of destructive confusion between them.

The impending loss of the farm and the wreckage of the family that has in fact preceded it are symbolized not only by this confusion but by palpable theatrical objects: first, by the splintered door that opens the farmhouse indiscriminately to the outside world; by the loss of Emma's carefully nurtured 4-H Club demonstration chicken; by the famished concentration of the whole family, but especially of the son Wesley, on the empty refrigerator; and by the lamb's contracting a case of maggots, then being nursed back to health only to be butchered in the end by Wesley.

Shepard dramatizes the destruction by manipulating contrasts between the children and their parents. For example, Weston has broken but Wesley is repairing the screen door; Emma wants to repair, Weston to destroy cars.

Ella and Weston are lost in an echoing grandiosity. They are addicted to large, hysterical gestures and plans: Weston totals cars, makes speculative land purchases like an investment baron, smashes his own front door to pieces just to spite his wife. Born again after a week-long drunken spree, on an impulse he grandly does all the laundry in the house. The same impulse sponsors his offer to cook breakfast for Wesley. Ella is similarly an artist of impulse. Though she knows it's her husband trying to get into the house, she calls the police anyway; only that dramatic gesture will do. As her son urinates on the floor, she examines his penis and compares it with her father's. She aspires to the "High art. Paintings. Castles. Buildings. Fancy food" of Europe (143). The wish to go to Europe separates her from her husband, who prefers the desert and Mexico.

In contrast, the children, at the beginning of the play at least, are sober. Wesley questions his mother carefully about her hysterical response to

Weston's drunken rampage of the previous night
(136) and exposes her impulsiveness. At this point
in the play Emma is as sober as her brother. Her
outraged speech on her mother's having boiled her
4-H Club chicken takes place offstage. Significantly, she cannot give vent to her anger on stage.
The speech is a comic gem, but disguised by the
comedy and Emma's tremendous volume is a sober idea of orderly growth and development, silly
as it may have been to raise a chicken for the
purposes Emma intended. She did, as she says,
invest careful preparations over a full year only to
have it destroyed in a moment by her mother's
thoughtlessness.

Not only is Emma sober but she is wise beyond her years. When Ella, the artist-mother, reveals her plans—to take the children to Europe "to
try to change things, to bring a little adventure"
into their lives—Emma's response is that the plan
"sounds awful."

> ELLA: Why? What's so awful about that? It could be
> a vacation.
> EMMA: It'd be the same as it is here.
> ELLA: No, it wouldn't! We'd be in Europe. A whole
> new place.
> EMMA: But we'd all be the same people (148).

Moreover, Emma has the right characterization for

Ella: "YOU'RE A SPOILED BRAT!" (142). Confirming her daughter's assessment, Ella can only reply: "[to Wesley] Did you hear what she called me?. . . EMMA! . . .YOUR BROTHER'S PISSING ALL OVER YOUR CHARTS!' (142).

One of Shepard's best critics has suggested that the "hunger" in the Tate family is a hunger for "selfhood, distinctiveness, satisfying roles."[13] Rather, it seems that Ella and Weston have found what might be their satisfying roles, romantic ones, but cannot enact them in equanimity because they are not plausible roles for parents to play. Nevertheless, or perhaps because of this, they have held out to their children the exciting psychological promise of these same roles: the high adventurer, the wanderer, the artist, what Weston calls the "escape artist." He sees himself as one of these, an individual of abnormally large size, perceptions, and desires: "I flew giant machines in the air. Giants! Bombers. What a sight. Over Italy, The Pacific. Islands. Giants. Oceans. Blue oceans." (171). His story of the giant eagle and the lamb testicles embodies this same notion of largeness in size and aggression. Weston yearns to be one with that eagle. Consequently, in the story he cheers the bird on, for he would like to be as powerful and impulsive as that eagle; he is, in fact, an eagle to Wesley. Yet because of his and Ella's inner desires the children have developed an inchoate hunger. Emma had seen herself going off and playing one of the roles before she fell off the horse in act 1: "I had the whole trip planned out in my head" (149). She would work her way along the coast of Baja California, stopping at little towns, hauling in big fish, learning to fix transmissions, and finally writing a novel before she would "disappear into the heart of Mexico. Just like that guy" (149; the "guy" is B. Traven, who wrote *The Treasure of the Sierra Madre*). The role is not much different from the one her father proposes for himself at the end of act 1 and finally adopts in act 3: like B. Traven he goes to Mexico: "That's where everyone escapes to, right? It's full of escape artists down there. I could go down there and get lost. I could disappear" (194).

But neither Ella nor Weston can fit ordinary parental roles. That they are the same in this respect is embodied in parallel theatrical action: Ella's entrance in act 3 resembles two entrances of Weston's; though she doesn't tear a door to pieces, she makes a terrific ruckus and winds up, as he did, sleeping atop a pile of laundry on the kitchen table. They are linked together like the eagle and the cat that come crashing to earth in their linked accounts at the curtain of Ella's Act. Indeed, Ella has little to pass on to her daughter that Emma can use. On the first day the young woman starts to menstruate, Ella advises Emma to avoid swimming: "It can cause you to bleed to death. Water draws it out of you" (139). Emma must also beware of buying sanitary napkins in gas station bathrooms on the grounds that they are unsanitary. But Ella cannot bring herself to attend to her daughter. It is always Wesley who is being asked to look after her—to see that she doesn't fall off the dangerous horse, for example—or to be highly sensitive to her needs:

> *ELLA*: Keep an eye out for Emma, Wes. She's got the curse. You know what that's like for a girl, the first time around. (155).

Perhaps because little that Ella says is useful to her daughter, Emma, unconsciously electing to avoid her mother, identifies strongly with her father: she imagines herself a magician with cars—as he is; she rides a horse violently through the Alibi Club, wreaking havoc there as Weston had done.

But neither can Weston stand to be the father of the family. In act 3, when Wesley tells his father that he has really left Ella and not just gone "off for a little while," Weston explains that "I couldn't stand it here. I couldn't stand the idea that everything would stay the same, that every morning it would be the same" (194).

Nevertheless, Shepard arranges an enormous

flow of sympathy for Ella and Weston. He understands the rootedness of these types of American
pioneers. What they are they have inherited: it is,
as Emma says, "something in the blood" (162),
and, as her mother well knows, it is a curse as well
as a gift (164). But the curse is two-sided. It has also
made artists of the children who inherit it. The first
moment when the audience is arrested by the play
is surely Wesley's stunning speech, very soon after
the curtain rises, when the boy's frightened-child
words gradually rise in crescendo to the yawp of
mature stage speech that is pure Sam Shepard.
And it is the starkly powerful stage imagery in
which Wesley is involved—naked with the lamb in
his arms; on his knees before the refrigerator;
dressed in his father's clothes; inheriting his father's curse with the blood of the slaughtered lamb
on his hands—that constitutes the complex theatrical birth of the playwright.

Buried Child (1978)

SHELLEY: What's happened to this family anyway?

The second play in the family trilogy was
awarded the Pulitzer Prize for Drama in 1979. It
was first produced at the Magic Theatre of San
Francisco on 27 June, 1978 and was directed by
Robert Woodruff, to whom Shepard entrusted the

direction of all three. In December, 1978, Woodruff directed a new cast in a production at the Theater des Lys in New York. The play deals with materials similar to those of *Curse of the Starving Class*—a farm where husbandry has become impossible, inhabited by a family whose ordinary relations have been cursed by centrifugal forces that have isolated each member from the other. But in this play the colors are darker than in the earlier one, the action more eerie, and the terms of the drama more provocative.

The opening curtain of *Buried Child* reveals a mise-en-scène that has the feel of an O'Neill farm play; there are "shapes of dark elm trees" (63) beyond the porch. On stage are a pitchfork American couple from the Midwest corn country—the "Illinois" Shepard celebrates darkly in *Hawk Moon*: "Illinois green lush wet dripping corn bacon and tomatoes the size of your fist fights across the table brother fights father and wife fights father son fights sister brother fights."[14] The man, Dodge, seventyish and coughing his brains out from killer cigarettes, is downstairs and visible on stage; the woman, Halie, is a powerful offstage presence, upstairs at the edge of the outer darkness. They are squabbling bitterly, but some humor shows through; the action takes place in the strange blue light of the swimming television screen.

SAM SHEPARD

The physical isolation of these two is reinforced by the tone of their dialogue—mistrust on Halie's part, cheap jokes at her expense by Dodge: he is too fearful to oppose her openly. Gradually it becomes clear that a disturbing domestic drama is unfolding. The disembodied voice of Halie first inquires, then scolds, threatens, brags, and infantilizes, while the blanket-wrapped skeleton that is Dodge can only dodge the blows. Yet the effect of this opening scene is soothing because the play appears to be a species of theatrical realism. But Shepard soon introduces symbolic elements that place the spirit and its manifestations in magic and mystery at the front of the stage, and these soon become a series of dramatic provocations.

The first of these elements is that Dodge fears his son Bradley will cut his hair while he sleeps, a metaphorical mutilation that is actually carried out on stage at the end of act 1. The second is the entrance of the oldest son, Tilden. "Something about him is profoundly burned out and displaced" (69), but in his arms is a load of fresh-picked corn from a field out back that, according to Dodge, has produced nothing since 1935. Then, as if to overcome his father's disbelief, Tilden dumps the corn in his lap. Bizarre.

Although Tilden is "profoundly burned out and displaced," the whole family is so mutilated, diseased, and antisocial that their story can only be told as it "moves steadily towards myth, and dim outlines of sacrifical rituals and dying gods begin to appear in it."[15] The middle son, Bradley, is himself mutilated: he has lost a leg in a chain-saw accident. Tilden, who has returned home for the first time in twenty years, is virtually catatonic; he has been in an unspecified kind of "bad trouble" (113) in New Mexico. And, of course, Dodge is clearly dying, lying there "day and night," as Halie puts it, "festering away! Decomposing! Smelling up the house with your putrid body!" (76). Later there is an exhumation of the actual buried child, a mud-clotted object that Tilden carries in from the rain-soaked fields; the purposeful, biblical rain, real and symbolic, has washed the earth from the child's bones. There is a reappearance of a symbolically buried child in the person of Dodge's grandson, Tilden's son, Vince. Halie tells a strange story of a third son, Ansel, married to a Mafia princess and dead in his motel room on his honeymoon, a military hero and a great basketball player. The dialogue reveals that Tilden was the incestuous father of the buried child. Vince breaks into the house through the screen door—a violent entrance that parallels Weston's action is *Curse of the Starving Class* and that Thomas Nash correctly sees as a

SAM SHEPARD

symbol of rebirth. This is followed by the death of Dodge and his displacement by an heir.

The extraordinary theatrical image of the corn is repeated when Tilden, later in the first act, spreads the husks over his sleeping father in a tender gesture of homage, identification, and fare-well. Corn is mentioned in act 3 in Shelley's reference to a photograph of "all the kids standing out in the corn" (111). All of this suggests the corn king ritual that Nash shows is operating at one mythic level of the play: an older, dominating harvest spirit is ritually killed and displaced for the purpose of promoting fecundity. The corn, which Tilden calls "a mystery" (75), is also associated with Tilden's incest: Halie does not want him to "go out in the back lot anymore" (77). For though Dodge yells that *his* flesh and blood is buried in the back yard, the child buried there was almost surely Tilden's. Dodge's claim that the child is his (77) or that the burial took place before Tilden was born (92) is mere whistling in the dark, attempts to convince himself of the truth of the lie. For as Dodge says in act 2, "It's much better not to know anything" (88). Thus his claims are similar to Tilden's that "we had a baby. (*motioning to Dodge*) He did'" (103). More convincing are Tilden's asser-tion, "I had a son once but we buried him" (92), and Dodge's series of revelatory speeches in act 3 from which the truth may be pieced together:

Then Halie got pregnant again. Outa' the middle a' nowhere, . . . In fact, we hadn't been sleepin' in the same bed for about six years. . . . It [the child] wanted to pretend that I was its father. She wanted me to believe in it. Even when everyone around us knew. . . . All our boys knew. Tilden knew. . . . Tilden was the one who knew. Better than any of us. He'd walk for miles with that kid in his arms. . . . We couldn't allow that to grow up right in the middle of our lives (123-24).

Incest is the family's dark, hurtful secret, but it stands for something buried even deeper: the curse of its mutilating habit of isolation and alienation. Long before the incest and the murder of the baby came the corroded relations that kept Dodge and Halie out of the same bed for six years. The possibility of Halie's adultery is hinted at in act 2 when Dodge suggests she won't be back that night: "There's life in the old girl yet!" (88). On stage the sense of rejection of children and aggression against at least one parent is profound. There is a general failure to recognize Vince. Early on, in act 1, though Tilden is home for the first time in twenty years, when Halie suggests the son will take care of Dodge while she goes out to lunch, Dodge is stunned: "Tilden's not here!" he insists.

SAM SHEPARD

Yet three minutes later, having seen him, the older man is saying, "Look, you can't stay here forever." Tilden has no such intention, but expresses the wish that had been available to him when he'd been troubled and lonely in New Mexico. What is needed is talk, the kind of intimacy that Tilden means when in response to his father's bitter "I don't want to talk!" he says, "You gotta talk or you'll die" (78). But as Dodge tells Shelly in act 3: "You got some funny ideas. . . . You think just because people propagate they have to love their offspring" (111-12).

Shepard doesn't say exactly what the forces are that account for this isolation and rejection, but he dramatizes the lopsided power relations that exist between family members. For example, they are all more or less under Halie's thumb:

> *HALIE'S VOICE*: I went once. With a man.
> *DODGE*: (mimicking her) Oh, a "man."
> *HALIE'S VOICE*: What?
> *DODGE*: Nothing! (65-66).

Dodge is capable of ritual anger only, impotent in its mounting, impulsive violence of tone because it is directed to the air. Dodge wants his booze—without her knowledge. Bradley appeals to her to have his blanket returned and swears—for the sake of assuring her he is innocent—he has not put his hand in Shelly's mouth, the impotent parody of a sexual act at the curtain of act 2. Bradley mutters threats against Tilden. Yet Halie scolds everyone cheerfully and equally. She would like to build a statue to Ansel, whose death marked, as she says, the death of all her children (73). Poised against this plaster dream will be the return of a baby's corpse and a rejected grandson.

Just as Dodge "refuses to be a father to his sons,"[16] his living descendants cannot resist aggression against him: Bradley mutilates his scalp, a repeated and symbolic wounding; Tilden steals his whiskey and digs up his sensitive past; unwittingly Vince comes home to displace Dodge and take everything he has.

The return of Vince exposes the family's haunted existence. With him he brings a girl, Shelly, whose ordinary responses make vivid contrasts with what is going on in the house and who becomes a passive player in the little encounters she has with Tilden, Dodge, and Bradley. Vince, ironically, tries to get Shelly to stop giggling at the beginning of act 2—before they enter the house— because "I just don't want to have them think that I've suddenly arrived out of the middle of nowhere completely deranged" (85). Expressing the estrangement gripping the family, Vince wants them to think "nothing."

SAM SHEPARD

When Tilden sees Shelly, though he is denying he knows Vince, he claims her as a kind of
mother-figure by dumping a load of carrots in her
arms; she holds them to her breast maternally.
Dodge had said that Shelly would get used to the
strange things she is seeing, and her response to
Tilden is just such an accommodation. But when
Vince tries to knock the carrots from her arms—a
parody of Dodge's taking the buried child from
Tilden's arms—she puts it differently: "I'll do
whatever I have to do to survive" (94). With the
nurturant Tilden she forms an alliance. They have
a "conversation," something he knew he wanted
in act 1 but has since forgotten. She gives him her
soft fur coat to put on and she prepares the
vegetables for cooking: "Now that I've got the
carrots everything is all right" (99). Their intimacy
is so well established that he can tell her about the
buried child.

It is Shelly's recovery of her self-possession
and her consequent aggressive responses in act 3
that unleash the buried rancor in Dodge. He fears
death and not being remembered. Halie has traced
his heritage "all the way back to the grave": "who
gives a damn about bones in the ground" (112).
Now he tells Shelly his side of the buried child tale.
And this, together with Halie's entrance, is

enought to dispel Shelly's fears. "You're the strangers here, not me" (121).

Vince, finally, is not a stranger. His return is the key event that causes a dramatic transformation, an appearance of spirit. When he breaks into the house, drunk and smashing bottles, he is recognized by both Dodge and Halie. For he behaves so badly he seems one of the family and Halie can scold him. He can then threaten to "usurp your territory" (126). As far as Dodge is concerned, he can "take over the whole godamn house" (128)—a miracle of change since a few moments earlier Dodge was accusing Vince of thievery. Now he can calmly bequeath it all to him, significantly naming in detail the things of this earth, then die quietly unnoticed. After his death Halie, at the end of the play, notices "a miracle, Dodge. I've never seen a crop like this in my whole life. Maybe it's the sun," she says, punning on *son*, "maybe that's it. Maybe it's the sun" (132).

Or maybe the miracle is art. For Vince, dressed like a cowboy and carrying a musical instrument, is a figure of Shepard himself. Drawn back irresistibly to his roots, the artist-musician must return to "a new thing with him," "this thing about his family" (86), to "every tiny little meatball town that he remembered from his boyhood! Every stupid little donut shop he ever kissed a girl in. Every

SAM SHEPARD

Drive-In. Every Drag Strip" (119). In short, he must, in memory and compassion, reoccupy the substance and spirit of the place originally in his bones, the place where he himself suffered another kind of burial. The danger is that he will become one with them, shattering doors and whiskey bottles and failing to recognize kin, leaving the real world (Shelly) behind. Only then, in lying down with the ghosts, as Vince lies down in Dodge's physical position, can he exorcise them in the act of making dark and bloody theater.

True West (1980)

> *LEE*: All these details are important.

The third play in the family trilogy was first performed at the Magic Theater of San Francisco on 10 July 1980, under the direction of Robert Woodruff. In the next two years it was produced twice in New York, first at the New York Shakespeare Festival in December 1980, and at the Cherry Lane Theatre in October 1982. A television version was produced and aired in 1984 and the play has been successfully revived in regional theaters several times in between. If such a thing exists, this is in many respects a "typical" Shepard play of this period. Although on the surface it is filled with the objects and requirements of realistic theater, it is dominated by the mythic, magical spirit, menacing and mysterious, that is at the heart of Shepard's writing.[17] Moreover, the work focuses obsessively on the West, on art and artist in America, and on the dynamic of family interaction within the family no longer on the farm. Recognizable ghosts from the other plays in the trilogy include a father isolated in the desert, a mother who likes to travel to faraway places, and a persistence of violent stage action.

In his stage directions Shepard is emphatic in calling for realism. The kitchen where the action takes place is that of an "older home," "about 40 miles east of Los Angeles." The set should be constructed "realistically with no attempt [at] distortion" and the custumes should be "exactly representative of who the characters are" (3-4). In fact, Shepard continues in his introductory "Note on Sound," even the coyotes must be the real McCoy and emit a "yapping, dog-like bark, similar to a Hyena," and must not imitate the "long, mournful, solitary howl of the Hollywood stereotype" (3-4). The purpose of this realism is to make even more piercing the powerful ironies of the drama that flows from the characters and the situation inscribed in it. That drama Shepard has described as follows:

SAM SHEPARD

I wanted to write a play about double nature, one that
wouldn't be symbolic or metaphorical or any of that
stuff. . . . I think we're split in a much more devastating way than psychology can ever reveal. . . . It's
something we've got to live with.[18]

The "double nature" is perceived at once, in
that a kitchen is to be the paradoxical site of a
Western showdown, with a good guy, Austin, and
a bad guy, Lee. Lee doesn't rustle cattle; he steals
cars and TV sets. Austin is no sheriff; he is an Ivy
League–educated screenwriter, not more moral but
more middle-class than his brother. But there is
bad blood between them, part of the split that
Shepard speaks of. This bad blood is manifest as a
territorial matter[19] and as a difference of attitude
toward their father, a drunken desert rat. Austin is
nervous over Lee's presence in the house. Lee is an
invader. Lee is intent on rescuing the old man;
Austin has tried, and now washes his hands of him
as a hopeless case. The showdown is only one of
the variations Shepard plays on the idea of "true
west," which is at once the title of a magazine that
prints Western fiction, a compass heading—both
real and metaphorical—a variant on "true confes-
sions," and, in the play title, a question—what is
the true West?—for which the playwright has
proposed a number of possible answers.
A central variation is the West as Hollywood,

a crass and materialistic haven for the likes of the movie producer Saul Kimmer. Like Austin, who refers to his work as "a little research" and "doing business" (14), Kimmer uses the language of business and success to refer to Austin's story: "I am absolutely convinced we can get this thing off the ground," he says, rather than commenting on its artistic quality. "I mean," he goes on, "we'll have to make a major sale to television" and therefore have to get a "bankable star" (15). Austin is not to touch a typewriter until they can get "seed money," and, to complete the rhetoric of anti-art, "I mean it's a great story. Just the story alone" (15). For Shepard a story without the mystery of its context would be a piece of banality. Hollywood and screenwriting and Austin as a representative writer are thus in black contrast with Shepard's whole conception of art.

As Tucker Orbison has shown, doing Hollywood business and making authentic art are embodied respectively in Austin and Lee, another aspect of the doubleness of Shepard's conception. Shepard's general procedure as an artist is to write in pursuit of "an event that's happening inside me," "an open-ended structure where anything could happen,"[20] with "craftsmanship [that] always comes from some interior thing."[21] It is to make use of "words as living incantations," for

SAM SHEPARD

"the real quest of a writer is to penetrate into another world," to make a myth, by which he means "a sense of mystery and not necessarily a traditional formula."[22] Within the confines of this organic and mysterious conception we can find Lee's practice as a writer.

It is Lee who speaks of writing with understanding, who knows that this "line a' work demands a lota concentration." When Austin calls it "a little research," Lee says "I did a little art myself once," then angrily refuses to speak of it—an attitude fully in the organic tradition of art as a mystery to be courted and not one to be spoken to death (8). It is for Austin to "bullshit yer way into a million bucks" (13) by talking his story into vaporous nothing with Saul Kimmer.

Lee's work may not stand up to the formulaic criticism of Austin—who, unlike a passionate artist, doesn't want "to get all worked up about it [Lee's story]" (24)—but it has its own iron integrity. Lee will not leave out important details, though it's only an outline. And he insists on his script having certain essential features—the horses inside the cattle trailer (the "gooseneck"), the running out of gas—as if the story penetrated a particular world with its particular identifying contours. Although he needs help from his brother in the conventions of movie dialogue, he insists,

UNDERSTANDING CONTEMPORARY DRAMA

You can use all your usual tricks and stuff. Yer fancy
language. Yer artistic hocus pocus. But you gotta
write everything like I say. Every move. Everytime
they run outa gas, they run outa gas. Every time they
wanna jump on a horse, they do just that. If they
wanna stay in Texas, by God they'll stay in Texas!'
(50).

When Austin says the story is "not enough
like real life" (21), that the characters are only
"illusions of characters" and "fantasies of a long
lost boyhood" (40), he is paying the work an
appropriate compliment: art is *not* like real life and
it *is* made up of fantasy and dream material. Lee's
work has all the power of the final descriptive
passage he dictates to Austin to end act 1, scene 3

So they take off after each other into an endless black
prairie. The sun is just comin' down and they can feel
the night on their backs. What they don't know is that
each one of 'em is afraid, see. Each one separately
thinks that he's the only one that's afraid. And they
keep ridin' like that straight into the night. Not
knowin'. And the one who's chasin' doesn't know
where the other one is taking him.' And the one
who's being chased doesn't know where he's going
(27).

Even Kimmer recognizes it: "It has the ring of
truth," he declares, "something about the land"
(35).

SAM SHEPARD

Austin, by contrast, is at work on a "period piece" and "a simple love story" (14), traditional formulas. Austin's conception of screenwriting rests on knowing how to satisfy an audience's expectations. When he finds out Saul Kimmer has chosen to "develop" Lee's work as well as his own, he howls his protest to the producer:

What's he know about what people wanna see on the screen! I drive on the freeway every day. I swallow the smog. I watch the news in color. I shop in the Safeway. I'm the one who's in touch! Not him! (35).

Yet none of these privileged vantage points qualifies Austin as "speaking from experience" (35); everything Austin says about his superior vantage points, in fact, sets him apart from a passionate involvement with life and disqualifies him.

Lee's story of two men chasing each other across a Western landscape, locked in a relationship based on adultery, is, as Orbison puts it, "an archetypal situation in which ancient conflicts are fraught with the terrors of nightdreaming: anxiety, violence, fear, the way lost and no certain end."[23] It is, of course, a mirror of the on-stage story, another variation on "true west," the story of brothers psychologically and socially different and at each other's throats who are nevertheless entwined with each other. Lee is, in a comparison that Orbison has shrewdly chosen, what D. H. Lawrence has called "hard, isolate, stoic, and a killer."[24] He is a rough-hewn carrier of the free emotional life, a coin the other side of which is the edgy potential for violence. The Western value embodied in Lee is autonomy: he needs neither Austin to make him breakfast nor Saul Kimmer to make him rich: "They can't touch me anyway. They can't put a finger on me. . . . I can come in through the window and go out through the door. They never knew what hit 'em" (31). In fact, if it's a question of big money, Lee can "go up to Sacramento Valley and steal me a diesel. Ten thousand a week dismantling one a'those suckers" (24). Lee lives on the desert, where he has acquired survival skills; he is what Austin, in his polished argot, sarcastically calls "a nature enthusiast" (44). The screenwriter is unaware of the deeper implication in this phrase.

For Austin is all civilization, as Lee is all instinct. Thus Austin is full of manners, prepared to make coffee, offer money, be reasonable. He resists lending his car to someone who might crack it up; his civilized position is summed up when he says, "I don't want any trouble, all right?" to which Lee's response is, "That is a dumb fuckin' line" (8). It is really the civilized environment of Austin that Lee refers to when he describes the "suburban silence" of a house he has seen in the neighborhood:

> Like a paradise. Kinda' place that sorta' kills ya' inside. Warm yellow lights. Mexican tile all around. Copper pots hangin' over the stove. Ya' know like they got in the magazines. Blonde people movin' in and outa' the rooms, talkin' to each other (12).

In contrast to Lee, who spends three months in the Mojave desert with mainly a dog for company, Austin goes crazy if "I have to spend three nights in a motel by myself" (13).

When the play opens, Lee finds Austin working by weak candlelight. Indeed, he does not really work but is "busy about" his "project" for four months. In the end Austin is fed up enough with this civilized manner to strike a bargain: Lee will take him to live in the desert and a profound psychological transformation will take place there.

Thus these two gradually switch roles. They confess that each had wondered what it might have been like to be the other—a dramatic preparation for the crossover, which begins when Austin gets drunk after hearing that his script had been displaced by his brother's. Austin goes out to steal toasters—another ironic variant on "true west"— and Lee becomes all work. When Lee hits a snag in his writing, after Austin refuses to write the screenplay and Lee undertakes to do it himself, they strike their bargain. For by this time Austin is desperate to dive down into the "blood" element that Lee's desert seems to him to be, a dark and transforming landscape. It is the last piece of authentic earth for a farmless family whose suburbia has not, as Austin says, been "built up," but rather, as Lee says, has been "wiped out" (11).

Thus in scene 9, in what the stage directions call "blazing heat" on a "stage [that] is ravaged," like "a desert junkyard at high noon," they are sweatily one, working at Lee's story. Even as they are, however, Shepard begins a subtle undermining of the switch. The agent is the lines they dispute: "I know this prairie like the back of my hand" and "I'm on intimate terms with this prairie." The first, which Lee has written, is a cliché; the other, which Austin offers when Lee objects to the cliché, is out of character. Both brothers are lost in the woods as writers.

The entrance of Mom does even more damage to their unconscious wishes for a transformation. For she brings them crashing to earth with her bizarre appearance, her flat affectlessness, her mysterious power to command them to be children again—especially Austin. They are little boys again, and the stakes of their conflict are, for the moment, thoroughly reduced. Lee talks about the

SAM SHEPARD

weather and Austin assures that he will clean up the mess. Then Mom introduces the bizarre idea that Picasso is in town, mistaking the artist for his art.[25] This is a powerful commentary, both on what the brothers are struggling over and on how the audiences for Shepard's art respond to it. If they are like Mom, what's the difference?

At the final confrontation Austin starts to strangle Lee, Mom leaves, and there is a final tableau of the brothers squared off against each other "caught in a vast desert-like landscape" (59). The last theatrical image stands for a compelling idea: the doubleness of existence is permanent. Both halves of the "split" are poised against each other; neither can dominate and become whole. Austin cannot become more authentic and emotional and unconscious, and Lee cannot possibly polish his rough edges and "turn myself inside out." Each must live as he is. The truth about the West must remain in pieces.

Fool for Love (1983)

The play was first performed at the Magic Theater in San Francisco, 8, February 1983, under the direction of the author. The production was moved to New York later that year, first at the Circle Repertory Theater and afterward at the Cherry Lane. Shepard prefaces the printed text with an epigraph from one "Archbishop Anthony Bloom": "The proper response to love is to accept it. There is nothing to *do*" (17), then prints in large boldface type before describing the scene: "This play is to be performed relentlessly without a break" (19). In Shepard's production two elements were predominant. The play was performed at a breakneck pace, with as much physical action and noise as possible—mainly the slamming of doors by May and Eddie and the bouncing of their bodies off the walls of the motel room setting—all in the service of the rarest commodity in the Shepard oeuvre, love, sweet love, passionate, mystical love. Shepard specifies in the text that the doors be "amplified with microphones and a bass drum hidden in the frame" (26). For a reader this presents no problem; in performance the effect is to drive a sensitized audience a little bonkers and dispose them unkindly toward what is said between long loud booms.

Nevertheless, the play is a major work in several respects: it presents the first life-sized young female character Shepard has created; it displays large portions of Shepard's dramatic gifts—it plays for "high stakes," to use his terminology[26]; and the dialogue is not just fever-pitched along with the passion of its subject, but filled with elements of farce of which Shepard is a master.

SAM SHEPARD

Love is hilarious here. There is, nevertheless, something simple-minded about this work.

May lives in the motel room. The first stage image features her body, bent nearly double in a posture of desperate emotional exhaustion, with Eddie offering succor. She has had an ongoing relationship with him—on again, off again—for years (or since high school, sixteen years, it becomes clear later). It is some time after their last breakup, and he has driven a couple of thousand miles out of his way to see her. They begin a low-level argument over the "Countess," with whom Eddie is supposed to have had an affair, the immediate cause of their separation. Although May says she doesn't care, she also promises "I'm gonna' kill her and then I'm gonna' kill you" (23). Now, however, Eddie has returned: "I'm takin' you back, May" (24); he has everything worked out: a "piece of ground up in Wyoming" with "a big vegetable garden. Some chickens maybe" (25). Although this makes May "puke to even think about it" (25), when Eddie starts to leave, she embraces him for a kiss—then treacherously drops him to the floor with a kick in the groin. Eddie is a stunt man and rodeo cowboy, a "fantasist" whose deal is to "dream things up" (26-27). Many times, May says to Eddie, you have "suckered me into some dumb little fantasy and then dropped me like a hot rock" (25). Of Eddie she says, "Anybody who doesn't half kill themselves falling off horses or jumping on steers is a twerp in your book" (30), while of herself she declares, "I got a job. I'm a regular citizen here now" (24)—she is a cook. Their interaction begins to seem a classic confrontation in the war between the sexes: the wandering, world-building male versus the stationary, nest-building female. The male is back after a spate of wandering, holding out the carrot of a nest fantasy, hoping to entice the female into this arms. The ploy appears not to be working. The characters are "real" and interesting—full-bodied, nervous denizens of the trailer and rodeo world of the new West.

Then things begin to happen that alter the neatness of such a conception. May admits she's waiting for a date. This prompts Eddie to go outside and return with a shotgun and a bottle of tequila. Their argument reaches a pitch and she tells him to get out. But when he goes, she is in agony, crawling around the room weeping and hugging the walls, as if her arms were aching to reach through and grab hold of the departed Eddie. And now a third character makes a contribution: the Old Man, who is sitting in a rocker on a platform down left, a presiding genius of the play and for a time a baffling one. It appears that he is

SAM SHEPARD

May's father; he tells a story of holding her in his arms in the pitch dark in a cow pasture, comforting her childhood nightmare. May needs comforting now and the association is clear. Until the whole of the play can be grasped, however, the Old Man is a confusing character, for in the theater it never becomes clear what Shepard makes plain in his printed text: "He exists only in the minds of May and Eddie" (20). After the Old Man's story, May hears Eddie returning and snaps out of her agonized body posture; she sits to drink some tequila as he comes in with a couple of steer ropes and starts lassoing bedposts. Several times in the play she will rearrange her posture to avoid letting Eddie know how she feels or what she intends to do.

Eddie seems to be in a lighter mood about the arrival of the date: he thinks there is no such person. He and May argue some more. He drinks more, backflips, crashing into the wall. There is another amplified boom. (The walls begin to take on symbolic significance: to Shepard, walls stand for entrapment. Thus the banging against and hugging them tell us something.) Tension builds. May decides to leave; she wants to call off the date. Eddie watches her go through the door, then follows her offstage and carries her back inside kicking and screaming. Calmly he puts his spurs on, getting ready for Martin, the date: "Give him the right impression" (36). But before Martin arrives, the Countess comes in her Mercedes-Benz to shoot up Eddie's truck and plunge the stage into headlight-streaked darkness. In a great fury May wants to leap out at her and "wipe her out" (41). At this point Martin enters, tackling Eddie and wrestling him to the floor under the impression that he is raping May.

During the Countess's attack Eddie is vehement that May must pack her things and leave with him. Her answer is no. They stare at each other. At this moment the Old Man comments that neither Eddie nor May resembles him—and thus reveals an Ibsen-like secret: that Eddie and May are brother and sister. The balance of the play from Martin's entrance to the final curtain is concerned with details of the father's bigamous relations with the respective mothers of the two lovers, with Eddie's revelation to Martin that May is his half sister, and with the Countess's final attack on Eddie's property, the destruction of his truck and the letting loose of his horses. The last episode leads to Eddie's exit, followed by May—leaving Martin alone on the stage.

The second part of the uninterrupted action brings together the strands in Shepard's drama of love, for it intensifies and gives depth and mystery to the full range of what Shepard means by love. First there is sexual attraction, what Ross Wetzsteon calls "freely chosen" and at the same time, paradoxically, "ruthlessly fated."[27] The Old Man's tale is also one of divided love for the two mothers: "It was the same love. Just got split in two, that's all" (48). Eddie's love is also divided; the Countess and May are cut from the same cloth, active, violent, intense, and May responds to the division like her mother.

> THE OLD MAN: (to May) She [May's mother] drew me to her. She went out of her way to draw me in. She was a force. I told her I'd never come across for her. I told her that right from the very start. But she opened up to me. She wouldn't listen. She kept opening up her heart to me. How could I turn her down when she loved me like that? How could I turn away from her?

And then the astonishing final line of the speech: "We were completely whole," (55).

In the story Eddie tells Martin, the Old Man was in a towering state of divided passion, a state that devoured him even as in his nightly walks he devoured the dark fields as he drew closer to the source of his agony. But May's tale is that her mother was abandoned, forbidden to come any place near the Old Man, that she went on a frenzied search for him, found him. and when after two weeks he disappeared forever, she "just turned herself inside out. . . . I kept watching her grieve, as though somebody'd died. She'd pull herself up into a ball and just stare at the floor" (53),—May's posture at the opening of the play. Her narration ends with the fate of Eddie's mother—a suicide. And, Eddie adds, to the Old Man, "It was your shotgun. . . . She never fired a gun before in her life. That was the first time" (54). In Eddie's tale, the Old Man has come off better, so the Old Man is perturbed by what May has said. "Speak to her," he urges Eddie. "Bring her around to our side. You gotta' make her see this thing in a clear light" (55). In both Eddie's and May's accounts of their romance it was love at first sight, the old romantic love of centuries—a flow of spirit across a space and then a passionate attachment unto sickness. "We got sick at night when we were apart," she says. "Violently sick" (54), just as she had said earlier: "I get sick everytime you come around. Then I get sick when you leave" (30).

It is a piece of family business, this hot, helpless, enmeshing, and eternal love. It matters not a realistic whit that there has been incest between Eddie and May. Incest is a metaphor for the spirit that has encoiled their lives. That Martin is an adopted child is another metaphor; he has no family and is therefore bereft of this love, incapable of understanding it. His being is wholly outside the realm of this emotion, and the great staid foolishness he exhibits contrasts him with Eddie and May. To Martin the struggle of May and Eddie when he arrived at the motel was something like rape—he cannot quite say the word—and it summoned up his blood automatically. But he is always either mistaken in these matters or incompetent. For the love that is on stage here transcends May's "You know me inside and out. I got nothing new to show you" (35). It is entirely immaterial. It consists of shared imaginative flight—art, if you will. When Eddie and Martin are waiting for May to get ready, Eddie tells Martin that he (Martin) is going out with May just to be close to her—that taking her to the movies doesn't matter and that after a while he needn't take her anywhere. They could hang around the motel and "tell each each other stories" (45), but Martin doesn't know any stories. Thus there is no chance for him to engage May's imagination. But Eddie is a fantasist, and that is superior to any other quality he might bring to love.

That is the meaning of the Old Man's parable of being married to Barbara Mandrell. And when Martin is left alone on stage at the end, the audience must understand that they have been left in that motel room with a kind of blank. Love has gone its unpredictable way, leaving the storyless likes of poor Martin behind.

Other Works

Of the thirty-five Shepard plays that have not been discussed in this chapter, a good number are worth considerable attention.[28] For they define the outer limits of Shepard's imagination, and the most important of them set the stage for the major works that have just been considered. It is too early in Shepard's career to define his "periods," but the later plays, especially the last four analyzed above, are clearly different in manner from the early works and from those he worked on between, say, 1968 and 1976.

The earliest plays are the two works first produced in 1964–1965. The manuscript of *Cowboys* is now lost but though *The Rock Garden* exhibits no certainty of style or character it is still a herald of Shepard's talent. The next three works, *Chicago, Red Cross, Icarus's Mother* and *Fourteen Hundred Thousand* seem to be related both thematically and by a forceful and formal exploration of the form of theater. They show influences as disparate as Joseph Chaikin's Open Theatre and Brecht's Ber-

SAM SHEPARD

liner Ensemble. Then, from the beginning of 1967 and continuing for a decade until the beginning of the family trilogy, Shepard was seized by an anthropological imagination and produced works of what Levi-Strauss would call *bricolage*, the putting together of a culture from its shards, works featuring magic, mythic cowboys and real movie stars, rock and roll, denizens of movieland, outer space and even murkier regions.

The Rock Garden, a little playlet in three scenes, features members of an alienated family portrayed in bold abstractions that are already theatrical to the core. In the first scene, a boy and girl sit opposite each other at a dining table dominated by a father, completely absorbed in a magazine. Nothing is said, except that the girl and boy exchange glances—this is their minimalist way of relating—and sip their milk until the girl drops her glass and spills some of the milk.

In the second scene, a boy in his underwear listens to a "woman," lying in bed, presumably his mother; she talks about various things, mainly her father, while periodically the boy goes off stage to fetch her some water or an extra blanket, returning each time having put on more clothing. At the end of the scene, he is fully dressed. When a man passes by outside (the father whom we saw in the first scene), the boy runs offstage. Then the man

UNDERSTANDING CONTEMPORARY DRAMA

enters, in his underwear, and takes the boy's place. Blackout.

The third scene features the man and the boy both in underwear in a living room on "Saturday afternoon—just after lunch, just before the ball game" (222). The boy "never turns to address the man" and, "out of boredom," nods out now and then and falls off his chair. The father goes on and on about lawns, fence painting and building a rock garden. The final speech is the boy's, a long, graphically detailed description of his preferences in love-making. (This is the section used in the revue *Oh Calcutta!*) At the end, the man falls off his seat.

The significance seems clear. The alienation of the man from his children in the first scene begets the boy's failure to look at him in the last. As the boy progressively puts on more clothes he grows up during his mother's meandering dialogue in the second scene—to be replaced by his undressed father, a child for the mother. In scene three, they are both children but the boy has a hidden maturity: his sexual experience, which knocks the father off his comfortable seat. The playlet is happening theater, anonymous in the way that Absurdist theater tends to be, abstracting its characters so far toward type that the individuality is hidden. Nevertheless, each gesture in this early work conveys

SAM SHEPARD

itself powerfully through the impact of highly theatrical images.

Chicago, Icarus's Mother, Fourteen Hundred Thousand and *Red Cross*, Shepard's next group of plays, abandon the subject of the family as well as most of the realism of *The Rock Garden* in favor of a Brechtian assault on the audience's wish to "identify" and to be carried away by theatrical illusion. The remnants of characterization in the early play are replaced by mimicry, by what actors call "indicating," or commenting on rather than playing the character, and what Bertolt Brecht analyzes as freeing themselves from that "stamp of familiarity which protects them against our grasp";[29] and by such severity of staging as turning their backs to the audience and/or speaking lines in unison or from books or under such noisy stage conditions that the audience is distanced from the actors' plausible lives as human beings. The plays project formal, structural patterns of metaphoric stage interaction—what actors do with their bodies, what they say, and what they do with objects—to generate meaning through having direct effects on spectators. The plays are, in Michael Smith's words, "operating directly on the spectator's mind and nerves."[30]

The last group of plays appears to be opening up a new and fascinating vein for Shepard. Recently he has remarked that in his early work he had avoided the family: "I was more interested in being wild and crazy. To be unleashed, to drop the reins." Now he seems to want to probe "blood relationships," a "mythology" that "has to come out of real life, not the other way around."[31]

He may, of course, be forgetting *The Rock Garden* and its anonymous familial characters. Shepard's restless stirrings toward his latest materials would appear now to be directed toward the production of profound American family drama. Only this time, the characters are rich and full-blooded, a mythology out of real life in another theatrical vein entirely. And we can only look forward to still another development in a major career.

Notes

1. Biographical details about Shepard come from the sources I cite, together with the judicious use of biographical/fictional reveries in Shepard's *Motel Chronicles*; the material is also partly corrected and amplified by a book published too late for me to make full use of it: Don Shewey, *Sam Shepard* (New York: Dell, 1985).

2. Sam Shepard, "Autobiography," *News of the American Place Theatre* 3.3 (1971)n.p.

3. Kenneth Chubb, et al, eds., "Metaphors, Mad Dogs and Old Time Cowboys: Interview with Sam Shepard,' *American Dreams: The*

SAM SHEPARD

Imagination of Sam Shepard, ed. Bonnie Marranca (New York: Performing Arts Journal Publications, 1981) 188.

4. Jack Kroll, "Who's That Tall, Dark Stranger?" *Newsweek* 11 Nov. 1985: 70.

5. Chubb 193.

6. Roughly the forty-first play, *A Lie of the Mind*, opened in New York under Shepard's direction in December, 1985.

7. Richard Gilman, introduction, *Sam Shepard: Seven Plays* (New York: Bantam, 1984) xiii.

8. Gilman xiii.

9. Sam Shepard, *Hawk Moon: A Book of Short Stories, Poems and Monologues* (Los Angeles: Black Sparrow Press, 1973) 55.

10. Chubb 204.

11. Page numbers in parentheses refer to the following editions: *The Tooth of Crime, Curse of the Starving Class, Buried Child*, and *True West*, in *Sam Shepard: Seven Plays* (New York: Bantam 1981); *A Fool for Love* in *A Fool for Love and Other Plays* (New York: Bantam, 1984).

12. Sam Shepard, "Language, Visualization and the Inner Library," Marranca, 217.

13. Gilman xxvi.

14. Shepard, *Hawk Moon* 68.

15. Northrop Frye, quoted in Thomas Nash, "Sam Shepard's *Buried Child*: The Ironic Use of Folklore," *Modern Drama* 24 (Dec. 1983): 486. I owe to Nash certain emphases in my analysis. He has shown clearly that underlying the action is the ritual death and rebirth of a corn king.

16. Ron Mottram, *Inner Landscapes: The Theater of Sam Shepard* (Columbia: University of Missouri Press, 1984) 143. This is the first scholarly book on Shepard, and I have drawn on it in so many ways that I cannot document them.

17. For the analysis of this play I owe a good deal to Tucker Orbison, "Mythic Levels in Shephard's *True West*," *Modern Drama* 27 (Dec. 1984): 506-19.

18. Quoted Robert Coe, "Saga of Sam Sheppard," *New York Times Magazine* 23 Nov. 1980: 122.

UNDERSTANDING CONTEMPORARY DRAMA

19. William Kleb, "Worse than Being Homeless: *True West* and the Divided Self," 122.

20. Chubb 215, 214.

21. Shepard, "Language." 199.

22. Chubb 216, 217.

23. Orbison 512.

24. D. H. Lawrence, *Studies in Classic American Literaturee* (New York: Viking, 1972) 92.

25. Kleb 122.

26. "Stakes" to Shepard is an idea of a play's quality, something the writer aims for. "You can play for the high stakes or the low stakes, or you can play for compromise in between. . . . But what makes a play is how true it is to the stakes that you defined at the beginning" (Chubb 199).

27. Ross Wetzsteon, *Fool for Love* 9.

28. The title "Other Works" may seem to trivialize the extensive body of Shepard's distinguished "other" work to be discussed here. It is simply due to considerations of space that I am following this format here and with the other writers discussed in this book.

29. Quoted Mottram 38.

30. Michael Smith, notes on *Icarus's Mother, Chicago and Other Plays* (New York: Urizen, 1981) 26.

31. Samuel G. Freedman, "Sam Shepard's Mythic Vision of the Family," *New York Times* 12 Dec. 1985: 2.20.

CHAPTER THREE

When the Battle's Lost and Won: *David Rabe*

Biography and Approaches to the Work

American wars have enlisted the imaginations of poets and prose writers from Walt Whitman to Norman Mailer. Now a dramatist with sizable gifts has come along to imagine the most recent of these disasters. Not only has David Rabe put on stage the lacerating drama of the Vietnam war, in which he was a participant, but he has followed with painstaking artistry the elements in the national life and consciousness that were shaped by, and gave shape to, the period during and after the conflict, notably the rootlessness, the drug culture, the obsession with mechanical sex, a general longing for something unknown but surely grand, and the inevitability of violence.

For this task he seems to have been well prepared by his particular background. Born into a Catholic family in the good Midwestern American town of Dubuque, Iowa, on 10 March 1940, Rabe stayed put in Dubuque, attending Catholic paro-

UNDERSTANDING CONTEMPORARY DRAMA

chial schools until, at the age of twenty-two, he was graduated with a BA in English from Loras College, a small local Catholic institution. After that, he left Iowa to go to graduate school and subsequently go to war to gain the crucial experience that enabled him to become the writer he is. Rabe's father, William, who taught history in a high school in Dubuque, had published a novel. Later, William Rabe was to work as a meat packer, thus filling out the contours of a career the order of which his son would reverse: odd job, teaching, publication. His mother, Ruth, had worked at J. C. Penney and seems to have been a spirited and independent woman.

Rabe was shaped by his small-town upbringing, developing traditional American values. Among them were the "toughness" that he would later see as problematic in the American male after that toughness had been upstaged by a new call for tenderness. Looking back on his youth, he describes the period as a series of tests: "walking a thin ledge, leaping across the gap between two cliffs, shooting birds and rabbits."[1] There was also playing football, about which he was avid, once harboring ambitions to become a professional. Along the way there was a tentative first struggle with his Catholicism. Rabe has said that these

DAVID RABE

pursuits required him to control certain feelings, "the feelings that you think of as 'weak.' "[2]

He has also remarked vis-à-vis this period in his life that "I never heard of the theatre. I was maybe fifteen before I saw a play."[3] Nevertheless, if life in Dubuque did not give him a toehold in the world of culture, it did provide a solid position from which to take an ethical view of experience. For there is something profoundly middle American and ethical about Rabe and his work. To give just one example, he might have escaped service in Vietnam but at the time saw that service "as a cause."[4] His view of things did not change until later—to a more stringent and no less American morality.

After Loras, Rabe went to Philadelphia, where he enrolled in a graduate theater program at Villanova and held down various life-sustaining jobs. From there he was drafted into the Army in 1965. His two-year hitch included eleven months with a hospital support group near Long Binh, where what he saw of casualties and of Americans' involvement in Vietnamese society obviously affected him deeply—so much so, in fact, that after his discharge he tried hard to get a correspondent's job in order to return to Vietnam, even going so far as to apply to the Hong Kong *Standard*. Rabe admits that the impact of Vietnam did not strike until he got home and found himself estranged from friends and family precisely on the grounds of having a different view of the war than they did. Theirs, he concluded, was a version of the conflict that would play on television. For a time, therefore, he was much alone. During one period he found himself haunting Philadelphia go-go bars. In those bars "there was the same sense of proximate violence and the same sense of indiscriminate behavior being acceptable that there is in the army"; a go-go bar was "the only place I felt comfortable after the army,"[5] Unable to return to the war zone, Rabe resumed his studies at Villanova and almost immediately began to pour his experience into early drafts of *The Basic Training of Pavlo Hummel* and *Sticks and Bones*.

Rabe had begun to write short stories and plays as early as Loras College and now, through a professor who liked his work, had the good luck to be offered the unused portion of a Rockefeller grant. The grant freed him to work full time on his plays, and the work advanced rapidly. Villanova produced *Sticks and Bones*. After receiving his MA and now married to his first wife, Rabe went to work as a feature writer for the New Haven *Register*. There a series of articles he wrote on the addict rehabilitation program at Daytop village earned him an Associated Press journalism award for

DAVID RABE

1970. Later that year came the breakthrough with the acceptance of *Pavlo Hummel* by the New York Shakespeare Festival. Yet despite the success of the play and, later, of *Sticks and Bones*, Rabe returned to Villanova as both playwright-in-residence and instructor in film history and playwriting. It was not until 1974 that he was able to begin to live on his earnings as a writer, and then, ironically, only because, having made his way to Hollywood, he was paid very well to write screenplays that were never produced.

David Rabe's theater has links with that of Arthur Miller, whom he admires, and with Miller's precursor, Ibsen, with whom he shares the moralist's project of exposing social hypocrisy. A fierce and scrupulous honesty pervades Rabe's work; one senses a punishing scourge moving through a corrupt social order. His themes are race, sex, violence, death—the intractable difficulty of ordinary male-female relations, the need for a pitilessly clear vision, the inevitability of uncontrolled behavior in contemporary post–Vietnam society. A particularly important element in Rabe's work is his depiction of the male world and of what it means to be a male in America in his time. *Streamers* and *Hurlyburly* are portraits of this world. Rabe also offers a devasting view of the middle class and its pieties; he is particularly savage in depicting the current dependency on television and how that dependency has lately underwritten and even accelerated the debasement of language.

Rabe is a realist playwright like Ibsen and Miller; his tendency is to direct his realism so that it intersects with the irreal and the poetic. Thus he uses impressionistic and surrealist elements—a muscial vaudeville on the conflict between the conscious and the unconscious, climaxed with an exploding set; characters who are figments of other characters' imaginations; mythological interpenetration on a space stage, and the like. Neither a notable experimenter with form—like Shepard, say—nor an endless duplicator of his own work, Rabe has searched for the right forms of ritual theater to embody his high sense of overriding purpose.

Major Works

The Basic Training of Pavlo Hummel (1971)

> ARDELL: Sometimes I look at you, I don't know what I think I'm seein', but it sooo simple. You black on the inside. In there where you live, you that awful hurtin' black so you can't see yourself no way. Not up or down or in or out (46).[6]

> He will learn only that he is lost, not how, why, or even where. His talent is for leaping into the fire.[7]

DAVID RABE

Kenneth Brown's *The Brig*, produced by the Living Theater in 1963, was a metaphor for the enslavement of individuals by the institutions of society. The excruciating punishment routines to which the inmates of a Marine prison compound are subjected and the style of the play—groups of characters together inhabiting collective roles, Brown's Marines the oppressed, the jailers their oppressors—drove home with crude power an idea that had just begun to dart about in the air of our lost connections: that life with any conditions at all was intolerable. Since society was full of conditions, it was inherently evil. This was an idea that would dominate the thinking of the young and the impressionable and contribute to the identity of a decade. In the fatal embrace of this delusion the Living Theater would take Brown's play and its equally emblematic *Paradise Now* and leave the country virtually for good.

David Rabe's play, produced by the New York Shakespeare Festival in 1971, is a work of the 70s and conveys a different idea: its antihero has no wish to rebel, has little self-consciousness, and is avid for the structured experience the army provides. In fact, what was punishment in *The Brig* has become routine basic training in *Pavlo*—in both the military lives of the trainees and their lives in the barracks. When Pavlo is completely "trained" by the army, he dies.

Pavlo, often grouped with *Sticks and Bones* and *Streamers* as Rabe's Vietnam trilogy, is as much about war as Shaw's *Arms and the Man*, in the sense that both plays undertake to dramatize attitudes toward a permanent social condition. Rabe says his work is no doctrinaire antiwar play and that antiwar plays have political effects;[8] that he was trying to make sense of Vietnam both for himself and for others. And, of course, his play is not a tract, like, say, Irwin Shaw's *Bury the Dead* (1935). The war here is primarily an intense backdrop to the problem of Pavlo's rootlessness and his desire for experience and direction. Nevertheless, the play also addresses the Vietnam war specifically; that is, it advances the idea that only the worst of us (Pavlo) was enthusiastic about it (and he wound up dead in a brothel, killed by a fellow American as a result of a dangerous division in human solidarity and communication); that the violence engendered in men at war had been exacerbated in Vietnam; that things had come to such an unpretty pass as this.

The setting for the play is a stage dominated by the drill sergeant's tower and composed of the ubiquitous slatted wood flooring favored by army barracks everywhere. On this platform the narra-

DAVID RABE

tive plays out the basic structural pattern of army life: eight weeks of basic training rewarded with a leave home, followed by assignment to a unit. The physical action follows the rhythms inherent in these elements—the rhymes that count cadence for the company's marching and singing; the calisthenics; the encounters with the drill sergeant and officers. The emotional action follows Pavlo as he tries desperately to conform to a code of conduct that everyone else does his best to subvert.

The play opens with a scene in a Saigon brothel. Pavlo is "fragged" there by a sergeant with whom he'd quarreled over the favors of a prostitute. The quarrel was a significant one; what was at stake was the sergeant's roleplaying with Yen, the girl, especially his repeated assurance that he was going to take her back home and marry her. She didn't believe him, but she was willing enough to play the scene. Pavlo, the nonconformist, was not. Insisting in his blunt way that the girl is just a whore and that he needs to get his rocks off, Pavlo issues a fatal challenge:

> *PAVLO*: I don't know who you think this bitch is, Sarge, but . . . I'm gonna take her in behind those curtains . . . and then maybe I'm gonna turn her over, . . . you understand me? You don't like it you best come in pull me off (105).

In the surrealist style of the play Pavlo wakes up in death to be greeted by Ardell, a shrewd, experienced, and soldierly black man whom only Pavlo can see. Symbolically Ardell is a wellspring of consciousness buried inside Pavlo, and the irony lies in this: that though Pavlo has exclusive access to the wisdom and fortitude of Ardell (who sometimes seems too much of a presence), he can do nothing useful with them. For his talent, as Rabe says, is for "leaping into the fire." Significantly enough, he also wakes up to basic training, and the rest of the play follows in flashback, until it ends where it began. This makes possible a set of bitter moral lessons: you can't escape basic training; death is the beginning and the end of it.

In the beginning Pavlo is foolishly eager to please and join in. He wants to be a "lifer," R.A. (Regular Army). That is why he volunteers for extra pushups and studies his "Code a Conduct" so assiduously (45). (Note, though, that when he asks Pierce to test him on his guard duty responsibilities, he resents Pierce's jumping from the first duty of a sentry to the eighth; Pavlo wants things to be orderly.) Pavlo is desperate to become an infantryman and not a despised clerk or medic because that is the "in" thing to want. This attitude also accounts for the lies he tells about himself—his car thievery, running roadblocks with the police

DAVID RABE

chasing him, and having the violent uncle who went to the chair at San Quentin. All of this is in the service of constructing a macho appearance.

Pavlo is contrasted with Kress, who reacts like any ordinary civilian to the outrages of army life. He complains. Ultimately Kress, of course, "fails" the basic training course and is "recycled." That is, he is denied the leave the others get. Wishing to make amends to Kress, Pavlo attempts a mawkish speech before the men assembled in the barracks, enraging Kress, the ultimate civilian. (As Sgt. Tower has warned his trainees, there is nothing lower than a civilian.) It is Kress who keeps calling Pavlo weird. And it is Kress who tells Pavlo, "I don't wanna talk to you because you don't talk American, you talk Hummel! Some goddamn foreign language!"(24). After Pavlo's speech Kress physically humiliates him, and Pierce, his trainee corporal, is so disgusted with him that Pavlo makes the suicide attempt. The enrobing ritual that ends act 1 flows directly out of this action. The scene does not, as Janet Hertzbach has suggested, parody the "arming of a young knight"[9] but rather an initiation into a comradeship of the very young and very frightened, a comradeship that relies on uniforms rather than individual identity: parochial school, boy scouts, naval cadets, or the company of servants:

> *ARDELL* [to Pavlo]: You gonna be that fat fat rat,
> eatin' cheese, down on his knees, yeh, baby, doffin'
> his red cap, sayin', "Yes, Massa" (62).

In his heart Pavlo would like to do away with all civilians. His ideal is one Sergeant Tinden, who, seeing two Vietnamese, a little girl and an old man, walk toward him and his patrol in a village, shoots both of them to death without hesitation, "cuttin' them both right across the face" (42) because, as he suspected, both were carrying satchel charges strapped to their bodies. Civilians are the bane of Pavlo's existence—everyone from the girl who calls him a robot when he's home on leave to his brother Mickey, his mother, and especially Joanna Sorrentino, the girl back home whom he longs to possess.

The thematic resolution of Pavlo's disorderly life is arrived at in his mastery of mechanical sex. At home Pavlo had been fixated on Joanna Sorrentino, who wouldn't give him a tumble and to whom his mother wrote, calling her "a dirty little slut." When he reaches Vietnam and is able to connect with a whore, his life makes its final turn toward death. His training in macho manners is complete, his self-satisfaction unarguable:

> *PAVLO* [in the whorehouse]: To be seen by her
> [Joanna Sorrentino] now, oh, she would shit her
> jeans to see me now, up tight with this little odd-

lookin' whore, feelin' good, and tall, ready to bed
down. Ohhh, Jesus Mahoney (8).

It is a weakness that this thematic strand is
scattered like so much buckshot through the play.
For example, Pavlo's mother—though it is not
entirely clear—would appear to have been either
madly promiscuous or perhaps even a whore herself ("no, you had many fathers, many men").
Rabe's attempt to psychologize Pavlo by revealing
the sources of his malaise in this way is not
ultimately convincing. Yet Rabe dramatizes powerfully Pavlo's reliance on sexuality in place of
friends, warmth, purpose, even life itself.

The flow of the audience's sympathy for Pavlo
depends upon his being as dumb and mistake-
prone as he is. And in choosing this particular
character, Rabe is making a major point: that
American culture first produces such pathetic in-
competence and that it then turns around and,
rousing him to adventure, uses his life in utter
wastefulness.

Sticks and Bones (1971)

The first draft of *Sticks and Bones* was written
immediately after Rabe had completed *Pavlo Hummel* in the fall of 1968 while still a graduate student
at Villanova. It was given a production at the

university the following year and made its professional debut at the New York Shakespeare Festival's Public Theater in New York on 7 November
1971. It reached Broadway, the first of Rabe's plays
to do so, 1 March 1972. There it won the Tony
award as best play of the 1971–72 season as well as
a Drama Critics Circle citation. It was subsequently
filmed under Joseph Papp's aegis and scheduled
for broadcast over commercial television early in
1973; but the network, under pressure from its
affiliate stations, canceled the broadcast three days
before air date—even though Rabe had dutifully
changed Ozzie and Harriet to Andy and Ginger
and made other changes that had been requested.
The network's rationale for the cancellation was
that it had no wish to offend the sensibilities of its
viewers. The wounds Vietnam had inflicted on the
civilian population of the United States were evidently still raw at the time. Doubtless this assessment of its audience was correct, but in any case
television itself was likely to be offended by Rabe's
scathing use of the medium in his play.

It should be said at the outset that the playwright's use of television's Nelson family is not
intrusive in performance. Reading the text, however, is another matter. There one is continually
faced by character headings on a page: David,
Harriet, Ozzie, and Rick, and the allusion can seem

heavy-handed. At least, this is the case if the reader is old enough to remember the saccharine air of *Ozzie and Harriet*. Despite this difficulty the choice was superb. This symbol of American culture colliding with the brutalities of Vietnam produces an extraordinary ironic texture.

For Rabe's play is about the falseness of the harmony and goodness that used to ooze out of the Nelsons, a lack of vision, imagination, courage, and compassion which he ascribes to the whole of American society. His special emphasis is on the encounter between that society and the special horror of the Vietnam war. "In any society there is an image of how the perfectly happy family should appear. It is this image that the people in this play wish to preserve above all else."[10] The concentrated effort to keep such images in place invariably prevents the acknowledgment of experience that runs counter to those images—bad news, for example.

Thus the Nelsons cannot believe that it is really their son who is being sent home to them. When the sergeant major enters with David and says, "I have your son," Ozzie can only say "No."

SGT. MAJOR: But he is. I have papers, pictures, prints. I know your blood and his (127).

In act 2 Ozzie will call the police and suggest

checking David's dental records and his blood type. Now David too thinks some mistake has been made and, as if to convince the sergeant major, he screams, "I AM LONELY HERE!" (132).

David's experience of the war in Vietnam has blinded him physically, but morally and intellectually it has opened his eyes. It has made him entirely unsuited to the ordinary lives of his parents and his brother. Those lives Rabe dramatizes with scathing satirical thrusts that only occasionally seem artificial or excessive.

For example, in order to preserve the image of the happy family Ozzie, Harriet, and Rick are all addicted to seeing signs of each other's happiness and well-being.

> *HARRIET*: How do you feel? You look a little peaked. Do you feel all right?
> *OZZIE*: I'm fine; I'm fine.
> *HARRIET*: You look funny.
> *OZZIE*: Really. No. How about yourself? (164)

Little exchanges like these are frequent, musical phrases inserted into the composition. Where there is the slightest threat that things are not all right, there is urgent and nervous advice from one to another that they eat, take an aspirin, or rest, as if the strain of ordinary living were too much for them and would undermine that fragile image—as

DAVID RABE

indeed it would, for ordinary living includes the imperative to face one's experience. But for the image of happiness, its signs are more important than its substance, always a matter that lies deeper than a "peaked" or "funny" look. David alone knows this: "We make signs in the dark. You know yours. I understand my own. We share . . . coffee!" (163). Lives dependent on signs and imagery are crucially contemporary and, as we can all ruefully attest, solidly linked with television, its products and its rhetoric.

Ozzie is forever fussing with his set—to fix the sound, get the big Sunday football game, regardless of what else is going on in the household. Rick is forever eating fudge and ice cream and other empty goodies associated with television advertising. At the same time an analysis of how the Nelsons speak shows that the rhetoric they have acquired from the tube has literally destroyed their language and rendered it useless for the demanding tasks of emotional life—for example, reconciliation:

> *OZZIE*: [to David]: You look good. Good to see you. Yes, sir. I think, all things considered, I think we can figure we're over the hump now and it's all downhill and good from here on in. I mean, we've talked things over, Dave, what do you say? The air's been cleared, that's what I mean—the wounds

> acknowledged, the healing begun. It's the ones that
> aren't acknowledged—the ones that aren't talked
> over—they're the ones that do the deep damage
> (152).

This is a particularly artful piece of dramatic speech: it recapitulates a history of clichés. "Over the hump" and "all downhill" are World War II phrases. Postwar psychological jargon yields "the air's been cleared" and the other phrases in that sentence. But the last sentence is pure televisionese, a product of "serious" talk shows, the kind that feature the expert opinions and corresponding language of Dr. Joyce Brothers.

As if to emphasize that experience is not being allowed to make its tragic impression, Rabe shows Rick running around with an Instamatic camera mindlessly photographing scenes that should, but fail to, engage him more deeply. The counterparts of this photographing activity are the two scenes that introduce each act of the play: children looking at slides that they cannot make head or tail of—including a closeup of David's face at the moment of his suicide. Another instance dramatizing this forgoing of experience is Ozzie's initial search for the causes of David's withdrawal from the family in the night David was conceived—as if the answer lies in the biological, a moment of destiny, and not in the social moment, a moment of choice. Ozzie

DAVID RABE

tries to give substance to this notion by recalling that David had been a mean little baby and that as a boy he had cut up cats.

Ozzie and Harriet respond to David's blindness, finally, by abhorrence at his not participating in the family's exchange of signs that everything is all right. His experience in Vietnam won't allow it. As Harriet explains, after days and days at home he won't eat and hasn't even shaken Ozzie's hand. They deduce that he must have had some sexual experience, and they blame his stubborn alienation on that. Their first idea is that the girl must have been—shades of Gary Cooper in Hemingway's *A Farewell to Arms*—a nurse, a WAC, a Red Cross girl, or a foreign correspondent. Then a more disturbed sense of race and sex comes to the fore and they pillory his encounter with the deeper source of their fear: "the yellow whore." This is really a way of providing themselves with comforting image-preservation, a saving of something vital in their egos that seems under massive attack. The whole issue is articulated by Father Donald in his second act scene with David wherein the priest undergoes an un-Jesuslike trial, enduring excoriation from the cane of the blinded veteran.

FATHER DONALD: The sexual acceptance of another person, David, is intimate and extreme; this

kind of acceptance of an alien race is in fact the rejection of one's own race (188).

The terms employed here—"alien race" and
"one's own race"—and, in fact, the whole dramatic issue tend to confirm Janet Hertzbach's notion that Rabe is assigning race and sex as causes of
the Vietnam war. As the playwright has said, "I
consider the root of racism to be sex, or more
exactly miscegenation."[11]

Rabe's sense of the unseen forces in the lives
of his characters dictates the dramatic forms he
employs. In *Pavlo*, Ardell, who is at once Pavlo's
wish and his destiny, is an invisible character who
exerts a powerful hold on the audience's imagination. Here the invisible one is Zung, the Vietnamese girl David has guiltily left behind. As a physical
presence in the play she gives the audience a
strong sense of the Vietnamese in that her small
stature and her restrained behavior reflect significant elements of that culture. Moreover, the suddenness of her appearances and disappearances
mark the movement of ideas—thought, longing,
guilt, desire, expiation, and the like. It is, in fact,
when she finally becomes visible to Ozzie and he
attempts to strangle her that the play reaches one
of its climaxes. This moment comes directly after
David has announced that the truck convoys are

DAVID RABE

now in town bringing back the dead and that Ozzie will accept the bodies into the house to become part of the walls and furniture—to become, in short, reminders of the Nelsons' guilt. The strangling and sexual assault on Zung that follows is Ozzie's renunciation of this guilt and is followed immediately by Rick's suggestion that David commit suicide.

David has also precipitated the irresistible suggestion by insinuating that he, and not Ozzie, is the father, and by encouraging the outbreaks of violent talk that his intractable presence has provoked in the older man. "In time, I'll show you some things. You'll see them. I will be your father" (210). David understands: "They will call it madness. We will call it seeing" (216). Rabe is suggesting in this displacement that the title of father belongs to whoever is strong enough to face life and learn its bitterest lessons. Ozzie has not been able to do this, and perhaps his insufficiency is made manifest by the references to the mysterious Hank Grenweller.

Hank Grenweller is surely a shadow figure—to use the Jungian term, an "other" and deeper self for Ozzie.[12] The references to him underscore a certain vulnerability in Ozzie. Although he'd been a bully to Fat Kramer, he is now dominated by the opposite: "I am so frightened that if I do not seem inoffensive . . . and pleasant . . . if I am not careful to never disturb any of you unnecessarily, you will all abandon me" (203). Yet Grenweller is also a source of strength, having given him not just Harriet but also courage.

Though *Sticks and Bones* comes out of the same well of inspiration as *Pavlo Hummel*, it is a real advance in Rabe's work in that it contends with the deeper forces in American society and does so by putting on stage some of its most affecting wounds.

Streamers (1976)

The final play in Rabe's Vietnam trilogy was first produced by the Long Wharf Theater of New Haven, Connecticut, on 30 January 1976, whence it came to Lincoln Center in New York. There it opened under the auspices of the New York Shakespeare Festival at the Mitzi Newhouse Theater on 21 April of the same year. Both productions were directed by Mike Nichols. Although *Streamers* deals with army life during the period of the Vietnam war, and there is considerable dramatic comment on the significance of serving in that war, the play is ultimately concerned with the larger issues of what it means to be an American male serving in the army—apart from the particular hostilities under way at the moment.

DAVID RABE

What is at stake in *Streamers* is what is at stake for men who leave civilian life to go to war. As the wrist-cutting Martin, Richie's gay friend, says at the outset of the play, "It's between me and the army, Richie" (8). The army, which needs a psychologically stable group of men in order to function properly, is by its nature responsible for disorientations and instability. That is, a heterosexual male entering the army gives up not only his physical safety but also the psychological safety that lies in the confirming rituals of his gender. Without the protection of those rituals, for which women are necessary, his unconscious emotional organization is subjected to the strains of being stimulated by other male psyches, the momentum and angular force of their needs. To protect his heterosexuality he needs to hold back. For the homosexual male, entering the army is also the occasion for a loss of confirming gender rituals, for which other homosexual males are necessary. He too is subject to the pull of other male psyches. To protect his homosexuality he needs to press its claims. The drama of Billy and Richie is governed by these considerations, and Carlyle's downfall comes about because he thinks he is powerful enough to cross a line that the other two cannot. For Carlyle, a black man, imagines that there is compensatory power to be had in exacting homo-

UNDERSTANDING CONTEMPORARY DRAMA

sexual homage from a gay white man. In these struggles a species of military heroism—purely psychological—goes unnoticed, and at least part of Rabe's wish is to pay tribute to it.

As the play begins, there is an uneasy equilibrium in the cadre room between the white homosexual, Richie, Billy, and Roger. This is sustained by the deliberate blindness of Roger, the black man, who can accept the presence of homosexual currents without being affected by them, and the suppression of his quick sensitivity by Billy, the white man who cannot. They have established an interracial friendship and are determined to see it flourish—even to the point of ignoring Martin's suicide attempt with which the action begins. But Carlyle is the grenade in this play, and his need explodes the peace.

Carlyle's detonator consists of, first, the not-so-hidden injuries of class. He and the white soldiers are far apart; that is why he comes to seek out Roger and is so eager that there be a bit more "soul" on the base. Moreover, Carlyle is stunned and enraged by his low status as an army recruit, by the powerlessness he feels, and by the absence of opportunities for pleasure.

> CARLYLE: Jesus, baby, can't you remember the outside? How long it been since you been on leave? It is so sweet out there, nigger; you got it all forgot. I

DAVID RABE

had such a sweet, sweet time. They doin' dances, baby, make you wanna cry. I hate this damn army (19).

Only at the end of this speech does Carlyle mention Vietnam. Then he does so with absolute pitch of perception: "It ain't our war no how because it ain't our country."

Dramatically Carlyle also functions as a magnetic emotional field; within him he carries the instinctual emotional energies of release, and those who come close to him are affected by these energies. This element in his character shapes the climax of the dramatic narrative. For with it he tempts Roger and then—through Roger—Billy to go to town with him in his "wheels" so that, as Roger puts it, they can "see if gettin' our heads real bad don't make us feel real good" (60). Billy agrees to join the party directly after Richie says that going to a whorehouse is "disgusting." Then in the last scene of the play Richie unleashes the violence when he asks Roger and Billy to take a walk so that he and Carlyle can be alone. But this comes as a direct result of the others' talk about the whorehouse. In each case a soldier was attempting to shield himself from unwanted stimuli in order to protect a familiar sexual orientation: Billy holding back from homosexuality, Richie advancing its claims.

Eventually Carlyle comes to see Richie's being a "punk" as the privileged condition of the essentially white cadre room—"that Richie the only punk in this room, or is there more?"(56)—a sharp contrast to what he defines as "the black man's problem"; that is, that he is too close to his essential nature as an animal: "It ain't that he don't have no good mind, but he BELIEVE in his body" (56). It is, of course, Carlyle who instinctively recognizes that Richie is gay while Billy and Roger spend most of the play denying it. For Carlyle, partaking of Richie's flesh will unite him with the others and wipe away whatever stigma has attached to his life. "Richie first saw me, he didn't like me much no how . . . now he changed his way a thinkin'. . . . We gonna be one big happy family" (65). Richie and Carlyle were both deserted by their fathers, and their stories of how they responded confirm who they are in the play: Richie fell down as his father charged out of the house with his suitcases; Carlyle scolded his and got the best of the exchange. Yet in the final bloody confrontation between these two, racism as miscegenation asserts itself in Billy, and he literally "finds" himself with the razor in his hand and thoughts of "nigger-this and nigger-that" (72).

The violent dramatic action involving these four is played out against the presence on the post

DAVID RABE

of two old sergeants, Cokes and Rooney. They introduce the idea of "streamers," the central metaphor of the title which defines the condition of all the characters in the play. Sung to the tune of Stephen Foster's "Beautiful Dreamer," the song is a relic the old soldiers have cherished since they served in the romantic 101st Airborne Division during World War II and the Korean conflict. It acknowledges that one's parachute has not opened, is really a streamer, a white tulip, "a big icicle sticking straight up above him." Cokes describes it when he recalls the failure of O'Flannigan's chute to open and how he started to claw at the sky with his legs pumping up and down. That image would apply to everyone in the play; like the leukemic Cokes, each is clawing upward with legs pumping but will simply fall down and go "into the ground like a knife" (35).

Cokes and Rooney represent what is in store for "lifers" who stay in the army (those like Roger and Billy, who keep insisting they're more regular army than the actual regular army men), a boozy camaraderie, focused on recalling the violent pranks, the humor, and the comic heroism of boyhood. Without real generational attachments to the younger men under them, they have become ambered in that lost boyhood. They wallow in idealism:

ROONEY: You just be watchin' the papers for
Cokes and Rooney doin' darin' brave deeds. 'Cause
we're old hands at it. Makin' shit disappear.
Goddamn-whoosh! (38).

Though they are bound for combat duty in Vietnam, they might as well be off to Sherwood Forest.

The fabric of the play is sewn together with the
appearances of these two—together in act 1 and
separately in act 2. Cokes, in fact, has the
imporant, and most poignant, task of establishing
mood, tone, and contrast after the violence has
taken place and Billy and Rooney are dead. It is
then that he is on stage for a long speech in which
he describes the "day" he and Rooney have had,
their game of hide and seek, his own affliction with
leukemia, and, most important, the idea of ripeness. Perhaps he might have done things differently if he'd had children. He would have let the
Korean enemy soldier out of the spider hole,
instead of blowing him up with a grenade. The
man in the hole looked like Charlie Chaplin. In the
end the enemy soldier would have been singing
"Beautiful Streamer." "Oh yeah; he was singin'
it." And the play ends on an extraordinarily moving scene of reconciliation, pity, and the ripeness
of experience with Cokes singing it in Korean.

Streamers, like *Hurlyburly*, is a play in the
register of realism, the stage medium that seems to

DAVID RABE

suit Rabe best so far in his career. It is a powerful and important play. And it would be a pity if it were ignored, as if it were as limited by its topicality as *Pavlo* and *Sticks and Bones*, for it casts its net wider and deeper by far.

Hurlyburly (1984)

An especially difficult play to classify, *Hurlyburly* might be said to follow Santayana's definition of life: comic in its existence and tragic in its fate. An especially long work, *Hurlyburly* was accorded great respect from the beginning. Mike Nichols was recruited to direct a cast that included William Hurt as Eddie, Christopher Walken as Mickey, Harvey Keitel as Phil, and Sigourney Weaver as Darlene. The play was tried out first in Chicago at the Goodman Theatre in April of 1984 and subsequently at the Promenade Theatre in New York in June before making a Broadway debut on 7 August of that same year. The title, taken from *Macbeth*, suggests a tumultuous, confused uproar. In the late sixteenth century the world was associated with sedition or insurrection. Rabe had the Shakespeare play in mind when he wrote and once considered naming each of his three acts after one of the first three lines spoken by the witches.

Thus *Hurlyburly* has much in common with

UNDERSTANDING CONTEMPORARY DRAMA

Shakespeare's play. Both take place in a topsy-turvy world where males struggle for power; both involve a cruel war against children; in one, Macbeth is in the visible grip of a powerful mother/witch (Lady Macbeth); in the other, the grip of the powerful women on Eddie—and the others—is invisible, and must be inferred from attitudes toward women and children. Only stage directions in the printed text are overt: "Eddie . . . has been reacting increasingly as a little boy. . . . He is far away and with someone from long ago" (109).

The hurlyburly of the play is organized around Phil—at the beginning of each of the first two acts, the stage is given over to a tale of his violence—the mesmeric center of the men's vicarious interest. On the one hand he is, as Rabe tells us, the Jungian "least," the needy, desirous side of the others, the "shadow" of princely Eddie and Mickey;[13] or, as Mickey puts it, "No matter how far you manage to fall, Phil will be lower." On the other hand he is a powerful, violent, macho man—a sticking place for the others' boyish fantasies of easy triumphs through superior strength. That he and his wife, Susie, are undergoing now what the others have long since undergone with their wives makes the outcome of his plight something they can predict

DAVID RABE

with the masterly self-safisfaction available only to the cynical.

Janet Hertzbach, in her first-rate introduction to Rabe, makes the important point that in every Rabe play there is a grenade—either a real one, like the one that killed Pavlo Hummel, or one in the form of a character who explodes whatever equilibrium he finds with the pent-up forces straining at his contours. The grenade in *Hurlyburly* is Phil. He is armed not with wire and gunpowder but with pure, highly driven, inarticulate need, the psychological plastique of the age.

With it he comes to Eddie because only Eddie is willing or able to engage the extremities of experience being depicted:

> *EDDIE*: I'm talking about a man here, a guy he's had his entire thing collapse. Phil has been driven to the brink (111).

Mickey's cynicism has cut him off from such engagement: "There's no traffic with this thing" (144) is his motto. Artie, by contrast, is involved with the Akasic records: predestination is his bag. Eddie is thus the central figure in the play because he possesses—as much as anyone can in the world of the play—the Rabean virtue of having his eyes open. He is clear-sighted about the sinister Hollywood types that Artie is dealing with. He is in some ways ultimately wise about Phil's dilemma. But beyond these things, he is the one character in the play willing to expose, by expressing, the inner hurlyburly that besets him and, perhaps more important, permit it to take over and lead him in his responses to others.

Rabe has given the characters dazzling things to say, scenes full of wit and electric interactions. In performance one becomes strongly attracted to the people on stage and ignores what is made clear only in a reading of the text: that they occupy a fallen world.

The physical world is the house Eddie and Mickey share. Metaphorically it is a clubhouse in the woods where the young boys can get away from their mothers and sisters and ingest forbidden substances.[14] Phil's entrance not only begins the play but also initiates the repeated stage business of taking drugs. This is a nervous pharmaceutical rhythm to which everyone in the house dances. Hardly a moment goes by when one character or several are not either lighting a reefer, snorting a line of cocaine, or (literally) guzzling from a liquor bottle. It is as if each character in the play could say with Bonnie, "I am a normal person: I need my drugs!" Neither Rabe nor the characters enter into extended moralizing about drugs, but it is clear that drugs are the palpable representations

DAVID RABE

of the characters' furious, childish need for succor
into oblivion. The constant racing about the stage
for various items from Eddie's drug box, together
with, for example, the repeated use of the words
desperate and *desperation*, are rhetorical and dramatic devices that seed the drama—much like nuts
and raisins seed a cake—and give it its ultimate
texture.

The world of the clubhouse is not so innocent
as the analogy would suggest. The principal psychological activity here is the attempt at male
bonding, with accompanying rounds of classic
challenges—who's smarter, more accurate, saner,
more successful with women and in business,
more with and without each other. Or as Rabe puts
it, "who's boss and who can be trusted." There is,
further, a denigration of women at every turn and
an almost anthropological habit of "trading" in
women: Artie provides Donna, pimping for the
others; Eddie provides Bonnie, pimping for Phil;
and Mickey and Eddie provide Darlene for each
other. Sex is mechanical in yet another Rabe play
and again, as in *Pavlo* and *In the Boom Boom Room*,
is paired with violence: as each of the first two acts
begins with a tale of Phil's violence, each of the
first two scenes ends with a mechanical sexual act.

These activities of the clubhouse have as their
goal the acquisition of a male friend, the one with

the most manna, Eddie, and there is considerable anger and irritation over who gets more of him. To the victor in this quest would go power. Ironically, in the end no one gets him; he's back where he was in the first scene: in front of a television set, only this time he's awake and with a waif of a girl asleep in his arms.

Eddie has manna because he defines and affirms maleness; first, in his opposition to home, domesticity, family, and women; second, in his habit of powerhouse intellection. He is the idea and ideal. Only Eddie is ever seen confronting an ex-wife, and he shares with the others his strategies for dealing with Agnes as well as exemplifying a code of conduct toward the children of these disastrous marriages.

In this male domain, however, children have been abandoned. Phil has been taking a drug to reduce his sperm count and thus thwart Susie's desire for a child. He has already abandoned three other children, and "I don't want any more kids out there, you know, rollin' around their beds at night with this sick . . . hatred of me. I can't stand it." (65). Mickey, Eddie, and Artie have also abandoned their children through divorcing their wives. In addition, children have also been abused. Bonnie's six-year-old daughter was forced to watch her mother perform oral sex on a stranger

DAVID RABE

in the back seat of a car; Donna, the sexual CARE package presented by Artie, is barely fifteen and passed around among the men; Darlene's abortion completes the strains put on the young in the play.

This treatment of children is a species of the larger genus of violence that Rabe has been at pains to dramatize in the body of his work. Under this genus, is the sequence of violent acts committed by Phil, from his entering first-act account of "whacking out" Susie, to his own violent offstage death. On stage he attacks Donna; offstage he attacks, in addition to Susie, the man in the bar, Bonnie, whom he throws out of her moving car, and finally himself in his "accident." Just before the accident the kidnapping of his own baby is his final assault on the values associated with women and the home. The stage image of the men gathered around the infant and the little girl defecating while Artie holds her is a precise ending to the scene of violence.

Yet each time Phil's violence is a subject of conversation on stage, reactions to it range from ignoring that he has made Donna bleed, to admiring the ill-provoked act of hitting the man in the bar, to denying that it was a piece of insanity to throw Bonnie from the moving car.

None of the characters has a sure moral register with which to move through life, and in this state of affairs each is a plaything for events. This is what Rabe means when he speaks of the "theme" of the play—"that out of apparent accidents is hewn destiny" (170)—which, he says confusingly, are in some way "the same thing." Both the words *accident* and *destiny* suggest, in any case, the absence of control; and in the world of this play there is none. Moreover, the death of Phil does not, as Rabe also suggests, save Eddie from being Mickey. It is true that at the end Eddie is not a cynic, but he is lost in his own way. Rabe may wish to present his final stage image, of Eddie with Donna asleep in his arms, as evidence that Eddie will continue to stay heroically in touch with women, what he calls the spirits of vitality and disorder, but it is hard for an audience to see the pathetic Donna as a well of stirring emotion. More to the point, though Eddie is willing and able to face the extremes of experience, something in American culture has him tied like a ranting lunatic to the television set—the antithesis of genuine experience in the lexicon of Rabean thought.

For television is here, as it is in *Sticks and Bones*, a major source for whatever is poisoning American life. It is prominently used in the action. It is prominent at the beginning and at the end; it is fought over by Donna and Phil; and all the men work in television or, like Phil, aspire to. One of

DAVID RABE

the best scenes in the play has Eddie ranting at Johnny Carson's anniversary show; the whole issue is an appropriate symbol of the fallen world.

What redeems the play finally, however, is the blazing vitality of its stage language. The characters are "desperately" striving to articulate what they cannot quite say but cannot stop trying to put into words. Thus the repeated "blah-blah-blahs" and "rapatetas." Moreover, although no character in the play is authorized by training or profession to be as eloquent as he or she in fact is made to be by Rabe's art, nearly everybody on stage is at least sometimes articulate, even eloquent, at the very least capable of pursuing ideas through a maze of qualification, hesitation, evaluation—in short through the mazes of mind, of thought itself. For example,:

> PHIL: Eddie, for god sake, don't terrify me that you have paid no attention! If I was thoughtless would I be here? I feel like I have pushed thought to the brink where it is just noise and of no more use than a headful of car horns, because the bottom line here that I'm getting at is just this—I got to go back to her. I got to go back to Susie, and if it means havin' a kid, I got to do it. I mean, I have hit a point where I am going round the bend several times a day now, and so far I been on the other side to meet me, but one of these days it might be one time

too many, and who knows who might be there
waitin'? If not me, who? (70-71).
EDDIE: I mean, did she have a point of reference,
some sort of reference from within your blowup out
of which she made some goddam association which
was for her justification that she come veering off to
dump all this unbelievable vituperative horseshit
over me—whatever it was. I wanna get it straight
(17).

The language also embodies the uncertainties
of social intercourse and how this uncertainty has
gotten into ritual verbal gestures: "Am I totally off
base here, Eddie?" (53); "Hey, if I have over-
stepped some invisible boundary here . . ." (95).

EDDIE: Some sensitivity is the quality a person
might have. Sure, I can come up with all the
bullshit anytime—some clear-cut diagnosis totally
without a solid, actual leg to stand on but presented
with all the necessary postures and tones of voice
full of conviction and all the necessary accessories
and back-up systems of control and sincerity to lend
total credibility to what is total bullshit; but I chose
instead, and choose quite frequently, to admit it if I
don't know what I'm talking about; or if I'm confused about what I'm feeling, I admit it. But this is
too much of SOMETHING for you—I don't know
what—so at least we found out in time. That's some
good luck (52).

The playwright has perhaps been too simplis-

DAVID RABE

tic in assigning the troubles of his male characters to swings in the temper of the times—men being asked to abandon traditional male roles have been cast into a kind of limbo by the gentle new roles they have been asked to assume.[15] Nevertheless, Rabe has gone deeply into the male psyche, a kind of heroic journey into a damnable underground place, where there is a pool of rage ready to be activated against women at the drop of a hat, and has come back with a piece of art. He has written what is so far his masterpiece, a distinquished contribution to the American repertory.

Other Works

Rabe's three other plays—*In the Boom Boom Room* (1973), *The Orphan* (1973), and *Goose and Tom Tom* (1982)—constitute a small body of less assured and less coherent drama, but not less ambitious in scope and intent than the major works.

Goose and Tom Tom, produced by the New York Shakespeare Festival, opened at the Public Theatre on 6 May 1982, the day the playwright sent messages to the New York critics disavowing the production.[16] Goose and Tom Tom are the unexplained names of the leading male characters. The play is a vaudeville show about a pair of jewel thieves and their moll, whose swag has been ripped off by a rival gang, and their diffuse and inflated efforts to get it back. But the energy of the play is really detached from any solid central dramatic concept. There are hints that what we are watching is a series of unconscious transformations from the collapse of the rational: gangsters with animal names; spectral, hooded figures and nightmare horror movies on stage; Lorraine, the moll, pushing pins into the macho arms of her two partners.

Very little in the play relates it to the characteristic themes or theatrical practice of the author. He has had it in him to reach for musical comedy before—witness the transitional forms he uses in *In the Boom Boom Room*—and he has a deft comic touch; but the grounds of the vaudeville are precarious. It is lost in playing out its theatrical identity rather than pursuing more substantive issues. Only the fragile Rabean notion of a male and an "other" seems to have dramatic possibilities, but the playwright never drives ahead with it.

The Orphan is a more integrated work in that it has connections with the sources of Rabe's dramatic inspiration. Nevertheless, it is a labored and portentous takeoff on a theme of Greek tragedy—the story of the house of Atreus—which attempts to associate the horrors of Greek mythology with

DAVID RABE

the horrors of our own Manson gang and the My Lai massacres. The manipulation of a continuous parallel between myth and contemporaneity, to use T. S. Eliot's phrase, is here unwittingly in the service of denigrating Greek myth. The problem is that *The Orphan* has not found a way to embody the parallels between the awful sacrifice of Iphigenia and the massacre of Sharon Tate and her friends. The parallels are insisted upon but not dramatized. Moreover, while Rabe's command of language has always been considerable, he has not found an appropriate idiom here. At one moment he has a vague figure named The Figure echoing a popular science text ("An electrochemical change in a single neuron—and there are some 13,000,000,000 in body . . .") while at others Aegisthus cries out "Bullshit" and one of the Manson girls sings a chorus of "wow." Rabe's need to draw the audience's attention to history's repetitions and time's lack of linearity betrays the failure of the play. Nevertheless, Rabe is obsessed here as elsewhere with the fate of children, war, and violence and the intermingled qualities of sexuality that invariably heat up with it.

Though flawed, *In the Boom Boom Room* is an important part of Rabe's oeuvre for the student of contemporary drama. It is virtually a companion piece to *Hurlyburly* for those interested in the

complex of Rabean ideas on men, women, violence, sexuality, and race. Chrissie, like Phil, is a
version of the "least" in a play where the counterparts of Eddie and Mickey, the "kings" of
Hurlyburly, are absent. Probably abused as a child
not only by her father but also by her two uncles—
three ex-cons, in fact—Chrissie has a powerful
ambition to become a dancer, to tap free of an ugly
set of childhood constraints and a brutal Philadelphia underside in the 1960s, but she is only a go-go
dancer in the nightspot of the title. Hounded by a
sexuality that is powerful but easily available to
others—she *can* say no but isn't sure if she *should*—
she struggles pitifully for understanding but can
get no further than a bunch of astrology texts she
cannot make head or tail of.

Chrissie ends in New York finally in the spot-
light, but in a degraded state, dancing bare-breast-
ed, and, says The Man, "she's been workin' real
hard all her life to get this just right" (94). Neither
a flirtation with lesbianism nor a struggling sense
that perhaps she needs her consciousness raised—
an astonishing, though haltingly articulated intelligence—can save her from what is an ultimate
defeat. Ultimately it is her inability to articulate her
need that defeats her—especially in the face of the
social world she inhabits, where men are dominant
and punishing.

DAVID RABE

David Rabe has been compared to O'Neill. Then again, all our gifted playwrights are compared to O'Neill. We offer no greater accolade. In the sense that Rabe explores with the same courage and with a sizable talent the haunted realms of the American psyche, he is worthy of the comparison. On the other hand, Rabe may be in a struggle to free himself from a dependence on ordinary realism. We may, then, hedge the comparison until we see him apply his indisputable gifts to the modernities of dramatic form that go beyond realism.

Notes

1. Samuel G. Freedman, "Rabe and the War at Home," *New York Times* 28 June 1984: 13.

2. Freedman C13.

3. "A Conversation Between Neil Simon and David Rabe: The Craft of the Playwright," *New York Times Magazine* 26 May 1985: 37+.

4. *Current Biography* 339.

5. " 'Boom Boom Room' and the Role of Women," *New York Times* 24 Nov. 1973: 22.

6. Page numbers in parentheses refer to the following editions: David Rabe, *The Basic Training of Pavlo Hummel and Sticks and Bones: Two Plays* (New York: Penguin, 1978); *Streamers* (New York: Samuel French, 1978); *Hurlyburly* (New York: Grove, 1985).

7. Rabe, *Hummel* 110.

8. Rabe, *Hummel* xxv.

9. Janet S. Hertzbach, "The Plays of David Rabe: A World of Streamers," *Essays in Contemporary American Drama*, Hedwig Bock and Albert Wertheim, ed. (Munich: Hueber, 1981) 173-186.

10. Rabe, *Hummel* 225.

11. Rabe, *Hummel* xxiii.

12. The "other" or Jungian shadow figure is significant in how Rabe sees the alignment of his characters. In this play Hank Grenweller, the other, is a poetic reference; in *Hurlyburly*, however, the other is on stage in the person of Phil.

13. Rabe, *Hurlyburly* 164.

14. Before Rabe came on the present title, the play was called *Guy's Play*.

15. Rabe appears to be excusing the moral failures of the males in *Hurlyburly* with reference to this social development. To get the argument in his own words see either his afterword to the printed text or Freedman C13.

16. John Corry, "Rabe Disavows the 'Goose' He Thought He Had Closed," *New York Times* 8 May 1982: 17.

CHAPTER FOUR

Theatrical Diversity from Chicago: *David Mamet*

Biography and Approaches to the Work

David Mamet is one of the stars of a muscular theatrical revival that began in Chicago in 1975 and has continued there into the late 1980s. Mamet grew up in Chicago theater and joined forces in 1974 with Gregory Mosher, who came to the Goodman Theatre as artistic director that year and who is generally credited with inspiring a large portion of the Chicago revival. "Chicago theater," says Robert Falls, the artistic director of a Chicago theater company called Wisdom Bridge, "is big-shouldered theater. At its best, it is very muscular. . . . It's not polite. It has rough edges. It's not polished. But there's a tremendous energy to it."[1] Though Mamet aspires to polish, this is an appropriate description of his work.

Mamet remembers working for a director at the theater in Hull House when he was sixteen. The work done there with Bob Sickinger, who he says "invented Chicago theater," was radically different from the theater with a capital T that was being performed "downtown." Downtown theater was "boring and stank of culture."[2] The only theater that came close to what he was doing at Hull House then was community theater, but that offended by producing "sex farces" on the one hand and casting the director's wife in Shaw plays on the other. But, "we were something new: we were the neighborhood getting together and talking about the world . . . no Shakespeare in Eton collars, no sex comedies."[3] Except for those inaccurate last three words Mamet was right about his own Chicago work.

Mamet was born to a middle-class family in Chicago 30 November, 1947. His father, Bernard (a name the writer uses in *Reunion, Dark Pony*, and *Sexual Perversity in Chicago*), was a labor lawyer and a man who paid close attention to semantic propriety; his mother, Leonore, was a teacher of retarded children. The Mamets were divorced when the writer was ten, and though he has been deliberately silent about his childhood, he has evidently been especially marked by the event. His sister, Lynn Mamet Weisberg, recalls a "fractured family . . . [that] had a tremendous effect on David."[4] Nearly all of Mamet's plays hinge on the opposition of two individuals, the nature of the rift, and the energy available for reconciliation. The

DAVID MAMET

toughness of language, irony, and comedy that play around this basic division may be related to this fundamental event in the playwright's life.

That Mamet's plays are drenched in the idiom of the streets, and have been since he was a very young playwright, suggests that his early education was gained there. The opportunity may have come when he was thirteen and the family moved from a Jewish middle-class neighborhood in South Shore to Olympia Fields, a down-at-the-heels section that the playwright refers to as "New South Hell." Mamet remembers that in this period he hustled pool and ping pong and spent time exploring Chicago on weekends, frequently spending the nights sleeping in Jackson Park. It was at this time too that his artistic vocation began to emerge out of a number of significant experiences: years of piano lessons, a stint as a busboy at Second City, the extraordinary taste of theater he got at Hull House, and the influence of his semanticist father. "In my family," Mamet has said, "we liked to wile away the evenings by making ourselves miserable, solely based on our ability to speak the language viciously. That's probably where my ability was honed."[5]

After high school, in the experimental 1960s, Mamet resisted his father's wish that he obtain a law degree and went instead to the experimental

Goddard College in Plainfield, Vermont. There he studied English literature and theater and wrote *Camel*, his first play, as a thesis requirement. In the midst of graduate study he took eighteen months off to study acting in New York—an episode that cured him of the itch, since by his own admission he discovered that he was "terrible."

Not discouraged, however, Mamet eventually was graduated and found himself with a permanent commitment to the theater. This was expressed in the formation of the St. Nicholas Company in Chicago, begun after a brief interlude of teaching at Marlboro College in Vermont, and at the Pontiac, Illinois, penitentiary, an experience that may have provided him with models for the characters in *American Buffalo*. During this time there came a a spate of temporary life-sustaining jobs—short-order cook, sailor in the merchant service, cab driver, caption writer for the soft-porn magazine *Oui*, factory worker, and high-pressure over-the-phone salesman for a fly-by-night operation that was selling land in Arizona and Florida. All this while Mammet continued to write short plays.

The plays were produced in Chicago, some by the St. Nicks, as they were called, others at the Goodman Stage 2, under the direction of Gregory Mosher, who would become a long-time Mamet

DAVID MAMET

collaborator. The turning point in his career, however, was the production of *America Buffalo* (1975)
in Chicago and later in New York, both off and on
Broadway. Although it did not win universal ac-
claim, it established Mamet as an important voice in
the American theater. As of this writing he has
produced more than twenty-eight plays and two
film scripts, and shows no signs of diminished
productivity.

Mamet's conception of himself as a writer
governs his themes and theater practices. He has
been described as a man never without a note-
book. He writes every day, and he is tirelessly
committed to practical theater, to seeing his work
"up on its feet." This was his habit when he was an
instructor at Marlboro College and a writer-
in-residence, briefly, at Goddard, as well as during
his later theatrical affiliations: first in Chicago with
the St. Nicholas Company, then as associate director of the Goodman under Gregory Mosher, and
more recently in New York, where he has become
an active member of Curt Dempster's Ensemble
Studio Theatre. EST has produced a number of his
works in various stages of completion.

This pragmatic devotion to theater, together
with his seminal experience watching the light-
ning-fast comedy blackout sketches at Second
City—about which he has said, "For the next ten

years, none of my scenes lasted more than eight minutes,"[6]—probably accounts for the most prominent technical feature of his work: a great reliance on the Classic French scene. This feature makes Mamet's work actors' theater in that it depends less on language than on performance. Things are lightly sketched in Mamet, and the actor gives his work its being.

The most famous element of his dramatic technique is a pervasive use of obscene language. Mamet has of course gone to school with Pinter and with Beckett, and his language has the minimalist cast of Beckett's dialogue integrated with the menace of Pinter's stage speech. The obscenity, however, is strictly his own and stems not just from an extraordinary ear. The obscenity is not in the service of a naturalistic surface. It is constructed in the service of his characters' deep need for concealment. As he has remarked of *Sexual Perversity in Chicago*, "Voltaire said words were invented to hide feelings. That's what the play is about, how what we say influences what we think."[7]

Mamet's obsessive themes are broken relations, the failure to form relations, the impossibility of forming relations, and yet the endless pursuit of these relations. It is as if his characters were possessed with an ontological weakness that

DAVID MAMET

can only be strengthened by the relations toward which they endlessly strive. One relationship his characters find themselves in—formed without the striving—is that of master and disciple, accompanied by an initiation ritual to cement the relation; this is often seen as a not quite desirable form of human interaction. All these themes are evident throughout his work. The master-disciple relation is especially prominent in *American Buffalo* and *A Life in the Theater*.

Major Works

Sexual Perversity in Chicago and *Duck Variations* (1975)

JOAN: It's a dirty joke, Deborah, the whole god-forsaken business (*Sexual Perversity in Chicago* 47).[8]

ROBERT: To hell with experimentation. Artistic experimentation is shit. Huh?
JOHN: Right.
ROBERT: Two actors, some lines . . . and an audience. That's what I say (*A Life in the Theater* (63).

Two actors, some lines, and an audience constitute the essential form of a Mamet play, and the form is first fully realized in a pair of short works. *Sexual Perversity in Chicago* was first produced by the Organic Theatre Company of Chicago in 1974.

UNDERSTANDING CONTEMPORARY DRAMA

Duck Variations dates from Mamet's days as an instructor at Goddard College, where it was first produced in 1972. The pair opened Off Off Broadway at St. Clement's Church in New York in 1975. The following year, they opened Off Broadway at the Cherry Lane Theatre.

Sexual Perversity in Chicago is Mamet's contemporary Restoration comedy, a ritual of seduction gone sour, where the highest value among the lecherous males is given to the size of a woman's anatomical parts, where obscene language is entirely ordinary, and where among both sexes there is a general wariness of any kind of sentiment. The word love is used in a more or less authentic way just once; after that the couple who use the word— Deborah and Dan, the younger pair—find their fragile affair beginning to fall apart.

Mamet's notion appears to be that the older pair have a decisive influence on the younger, for they represent hardened attitudes of permanent hostility between the sexes (can this be the major "sexual perversity" of the title?). Bernie and Joan are both frightened of any straightforward contact. Joan's fear takes the form of a thoroughgoing cynicism and a perverse prudishness. She is automatically certain that Bernie is up to no good, in the singles bars, and that no good can come of Deborah's developing romance with Dan ("I give you two months" 48). She is also certain that her little nursery school charges who play "doctor" have committed enough of a transgression that she must call their parents and tell on the poor tykes. This fear is connected to her view of women, which is contained in the story she tells the children: "for one half of the day" a woman must be this old hag.

Bernie's fear takes the form of an implacable vulgarity and cynicism about and toward women. His two main principles are that "The Way to Get Laid is to Treat 'em Like Shit," and "nothing makes you so attractive to the opposite sex as getting your rocks off on a regular basis" (22). But neither of these principles works for him—witness the encounter with Joan—though he insists he is a high "scorer": he has done it on a plane, underwater, in a movie, and with a woman chained to a radiator. As Stephen Gale has noted, the theme of the play is failure to trust the opposite sex—surely another sexual perversity—and this has made Bernie into a model of certainty.[9] Not trusting women, he has created a mythology that accounts for their perversity, which is their enormous attractiveness and his utter inability to have authentic relations with them. In this mythology, he has an unshakable belief. Nevertheless, he wants—indeed is obsessed with—women.

Mamet has chosen well a breezy comic form as an ironic contrast to the seriousness of his material; the play is made up of a series of blackout sketches, the most important of which employ either ritual forms of sexual encounter and expression or old dirty jokes or some combination of these.

The first two scenes make use of the dirty joke. The first is a ritual occasion. It is late Saturday night in the summer in a Chicago bar, that time when the males gather to total up the night's score: "So how'd you do last night?" (9). What follows Dan's question is Bernie's story of the voluptuous young pervert who sets fire to the hotel room as he and the girl are about to consummate their lovemaking. Bernie's story is an old dirty joke, and the telling—as well as the cadenced responding by Dan—expresses his and Dan's submission to the large forces of perverse sexuality that are the norm in their social group. Thus in the story, although Bernie begins things, the woman is the aggressor in the sexual part of the encounter. Throughout the play women's aggression is emphasized. In fact, they cause trouble just by being there, as in the final scene on the beach. If it weren't for them, the men could go about their ordinary business.

> *BERNIE*: Lying all over the beach, flaunting their bodies. . . . I mean who . . . do they think they

DAVID MAMET

are. . . . I come to the beach with a friend to get
some sun and watch the action and . . . (68).

It is important that the girl in Bernie's story is
very young, a teen-ager, in fact, and that her
anatomical proportions are generous. She is of
course a comic pervert, but the flames she produces and the air force flak suit she wears symbol-
ize uncontrollable passion (and perhaps anger and
aggression) as well as high-flying genitality. Bernie
can only enter her through "flaps" in the suit—no
flyer, he. In the end, though Bernie is willing to go
BOOM, he is, when the girl commands him "now,
give it to me now" (17), unwilling. The moment of
warring passion passes him by, and only the
daredevil fireman can handle her. Danny's final
comment on the episode, "Nobody does it nor-
mally anymore" (17), while intended to apply to
the girl in the flak suit, can apply to Bernie as well.

The next scene, introducing the two women in
the play, is, by comparison, over before it can get
going. Only a teasing glimpse of the women is
given because such a brief glimpse is a measure of
their relative lack of importance in the scheme of
the play. Yet their brief dialogue constitutes an old
risqué joke:

JOAN: Men.
DEBORAH: Yup.

JOAN: They're all after only one thing.
DEBORAH: Yes. I know. (Pause.)
JOAN: But it's never the same thing. BLACKOUT
(18).

In a Restoration comedy the lasciviousness is
played out against a dramatization of the full range
of social life. In this way the audience sees how the
mesmeric pull of seduction and lust works out in
the rich context of money, manners, marriage, and
whole psychological aspects of character such as
envy and indifference, intelligence and stupidity,
the energetic and the phlegmatic. In Mamet's play,
however, there is only foreground, so to speak.
Mamet has focused his play purely on ritual lusting
because he sees contemporary life as eroticized,
unmediated by anything else.

There is something chilling about the play,
though it is funny and, at times, even moving.
Stage images like lonely Bernie, transfixed by the
television speaking to him with sex-obsessed,
wisecracking voice; the story of King Farouk's
lovemaking; and the final images of Bernie and
Dan, bitter on the beach—these create an impression that some saving grace has been savagely
annihilated.

Mamet has been justly praised for his realism,
but he is also capable of making a play out of the
most abstract materials, as *Duck Variations* attests.

DAVID MAMET

It is a series of exchanges on epistemology—what is known about what by whom and on what authority—carried on between two men in their sixties, the extent of whose knowledge on most subjects has been gathered from such sources as *The Reader's Digest* (110), "some guide to France," and "somewhere" (113). The men are prompted to begin their dialogue by what the setting, a park on a big city lake, enables them to see. Thus the central piece of arcane knowledge that Emil and George bat around is everything you always wanted to know about ducks—and much more, in fact.

Invariably what both men have to say about ducks is a compromise: a duck does not necessarily "find a mate and cleave into her until death does him part" (112) . Moreover, they are not "trained" at birth to "follow their mother" (88), but rather learn to follow the first large object they see—even if it's a balloon. But it hardly matters that the knowledge of ducks is unreliable. Truth or falsity are not issues here, and all the talk about ducks and associated matters only occasions for dramatic action with other focuses.

First, the discussions are occasions for allegories on the meaning of existence, for the play insists that there *is* meaning:

EMIL: *Nothing* is for nothing.
GEORGE: Too true.
EMIL: Everything has got a purpose.
GEORGE: True.
EMIL: Every blessed thing (86).

Second, the homilies and the allegories are not nearly as interesting as the ultimate connections between Emil and George—nor are they meant to be. Rarely do Emil and George engage in intensities of emotion or particularities of character development. These two are not so much individual characters as they are types—two garrulous, elderly men defining their existence by alternating role playing. It is this role playing that underwrites their energetic involvement with the topics of experience. In this sense the play owes something to Albee's *Zoo Story* (1959) and its very different tones of park-bench philosophy.

Occasionally there is a challenging outburst from one or the other that is readily taken up by his companion:

GEORGE: You started it.
EMIL: I beg to differ.
GEORGE: Go right ahead.
EMIL: All right, I *do* differ.
GEORGE: It makes no difference. I was holding an intelligent conversation and then you came along (112).

DAVID MAMET

The play takes its effect through the medium of these exchanges. And this dramatic construction is solid enough without the comments in the seventh variation on the value of friendship and the impossibility of life in isolation. For it is the quality of the exchanges between the characters that articulates what they mean to each other. They finish each other's sentences, helping each other toward satisfying wholeness of thought; they act as kind of amen chorus for each other, affirming with strings of interwoven yeses the speculations of the other on any given subject; they behave ultimately with immensely moving courtesy toward each other, and even when one is heatedly certain that the other is wrong this attitude prevails.

In the sixth variation, George declares that "life is a lot simpler than many people would like us to believe" (94). What many people would probably like is to persuade these two that discourse is trivial. But they seem to know better, and therein lies the central touching element in the play.

American Buffalo (1977)

With *American Buffalo*, his first play to reach Broadway, came Mamet's rise to prominence as a playwright. The work had been first produced in November, 1975, at the Goodman Theatre in Chicago, then moved to St. Clement's Off Off Broadway, in February 1976. A year later it opened On Broadway at the Ethel Barrymore Theatre. Ulu Grosbard's austerely controlled production earned it the New York Drama Critics' Circle award as the best play of 1977 and won Mamet an Obie as best playwright. *American Buffalo* has been frequently revived, most notably in a production with Al Pacino as Teach in New York in 1980.

Unlike most Mamet plays this one starts out as if it might develop a plot. Don and Bob plan to be partners in a crime in which Bob is to do the actual breaking and entering. The victim is to be a man who had earlier come into Don's Resale Shop—as Don's broken-down junk shop is called—and bought a buffalo head nickel. Don thinks the man owns a valuable coin collection, and because Bob has seen the man leave his house with a suitcase, Bob can break in to the empty apartment and steal the coins. But Teach, a poker-playing crony of Don's, persuades Don that Bob is neither experienced nor strong enough for the job. Bob is dropped as a partner; Fletcher, a character who never appears on stage, the man who won four hundred dollars playing poker in the shop the night before, is added to the crew at Don's insistence, and act 1 ends on that note.

Act 2 begins as the conspirators are gathering

DAVID MAMET

to undertake the crime. But it never comes off. Teach is late, and Fletcher never shows up because his jaw has been broken by muggers. The news is brought by Bob, whom both Don and Teach have gone to some pains to get rid of and whom they are chagrined to see again. In the course of a paranoid session Bob undergoes inquisition. When Teach realizes that Bob hadn't seen the man leave with a suitcase after all, he flies into a rage and slugs Bob, trashes Don's shop, and is himself slugged by Don. The play ends as Don and Teach take a bleeding Bob to the hospital.

There is no real resolution to the plot, but this hardly matters. The center of interest in the play is what impressed the critics in 1975: the dialogue that is artfully idiomatic for the milieu it represents; a relentlessly obscene language that also catches perfectly the ebb and flow of the psychological currents that animate the stage; and the psychological interplay between the characters.

Like *Glengarry Glen Ross*, *American Buffalo* is linked in the author's mind with a critique of the American business ethic. Mamet has said that his lower-class hoodlums are similar in aspiration and tactics to higher-level corporate pirates.[10] But the equation is harder to take here than in *Glengarry Glen Ross*.

It is true that Teach's attitude toward the

planned burglary contains elements of corporate discipline: he wants a crash course in identifying coins; he wants to "plan this out"—"Let's not be loose on this." Nevertheless Teach is ironically inept as a burglar—corporate ideals or no:

> *DON*: How are you getting in the house?
> *TEACH*: The house?
> *DON*: Yeah.
> *TEACH*: Aah, you go in through a window they left open, something (41).

If not the window, he goes on, "something else . . . we'll see when we get there." In act 2 he comes to the highly unbusinesslike conclusion that if the loot is in a safe, he'll simply look around the apartment and within fifteen minutes find the combination which the owner has conveniently written down on a scrap of paper and left in some obvious place. Both Don and Teach use the word *business* frequently, but the play is only marginally about business. Business here seems to mean something like being tough and clearheaded about the world and what one has to do to get along in it. Basically the characters are less businesslike than incorrigibly criminal or ignorant. The business world to which, as Americans, they might legitimately aspire is beyond them. They are inflexible, bossy, and superstitious, and Mamet is more inter-

DAVID MAMET

ested in how they respond to one another than in anything else.

Thus the major focus of the play is the shifting attempts at bonding between the characters and what such bonding means to the characters. As in all Mamet plays trying to get together is everything, and every play is a map of those attempts. This play begins with one bond in place: that between Don and Bob, a junkie, who is described as Don's "gofer." Don displays an avuncular affection for Bob but is a hard taskmaster, holding out to him for emulation the macho "business" virtues of aggression and self-reliance, the kind he ascribes to Fletcher: "You take him and put him down in some strange town with just a nickel in his pocket, and by nightfall he'll have that town by the balls. This is not talk, Bob, this is action" (6). Action, control over the world, is the primary virtue: "Action talks and bullshit walks"(5).

In a way Don is the master and Bob the disciple. Don is the supervisor of the younger man's initiation—as Bernie is to Dan in *Sexual Perversity*, Robert tries to be to John in *A Life in the Theatre*, and Emil and George are to each other in *Duck Variations*. Thus Don also preaches to Bob on the high value of friendship and defines busines as "people taking care of themselves"; but "there's business and there's friendship" (8). Though it is never stated directly, Don would like to define friendship as "people taking care of each other," but he cannot. The play won't let him. In the end he is touched by Bob's having bought the nickel for him and hits Teach in a fury at the young man's injury. Teach too advances the value of friendship, and his entrance changes the tone of what is going on, for he enters in a rage at the failure of friendly reciprocity on the part of two women members of the milieu, Ruthie and Grace. Teach now engages in an effort to ally himself with Bob. Sensing this, Don springs for the coffee and Danish—the supplying of food acting as a healing gesture.

Teach aggressively tries to alter the pattern of relationships and trust that he finds in the shop. He succeeds in persuading Don to sever Bob's connection with the impending heist but is frustrated when Don insists on bringing in Fletcher. Thus in act 2, when Fletcher fails to show up, Teach begins a paranoid campaign to discredit him—even going so far as to swear that he had cheated at cards the night before. That Teach finds Bob at the shop when he arrives only fuels his paranoia and drives him forward in his ultimate quest: the confidence and trust of Don and a singular alliance with him. That's why the only overtly emotional things he says are directed to Don: "Are you mad at me?" (82). At least part of

DAVID MAMET

Teach's rage is directed at Ruthie and Grace because they are together.

The coin with which Teach tries to pay for the alliance with Don is an assumed superiority in logic, reason, and knowledge. Through the obscenity of the language and the rhythms of his street talk, Teach puts on a careful accent of rationality and tries to be meticulous in arguing about everything, especially Bob's unsuitability for the robbery.

Fifty percent of some money is better than ninety percent of some broken toaster that you're gonna have, you send the kid in. (Which is providing he don't trip the alarm in the first place. . . .) (32).

Don's ritual response speaks of his wish never to be thought to foolishly oppose irrefutable logic. He too pays homage to this assumed rationality. It is all in the service of restoring what the characters lack: competence and control over their world.

When Teach trashes Don's shop, the rage he releases is triggered by the failure of this control. The whole fragile edifice that he and Don have built had been made stronger, he believed, when he had gotten rid of the weak and incompetent Bob. Ironically enough, Bob's weakness had been at the heart of the caper: to please Don he had lied about the possibility of stealing the coins.

The title suggests a vanished herd roaming the plains near where Chicago stands now—immensely powerful beasts, perhaps like the powerful urban beasts walking the outlands of the city. Powerful as the buffalo were, however, they had no control over their fates, and in this sense the title is appropriate to the men in Don's Resale Shop.

A Life in the Theatre (1977)

Like much of Mamet's work, *A Life in the Theatre* was first produced at the Goodman Theatre in Chicago, where it opened on 4 February 1977. A new production was mounted Off Broadway at the Theater des Lys in New York on 20 October 1977 and met with enthusiastic critical reception. It was the first of Mamet's plays to be made into a film and was telecast on 27 June 1979.

The materials of the play come from Mamet's considerable experience in the theater and show a shrewd and tactful command of that world. In typical Mamet fashion the play lives on its short scenes. There are twenty-six of them, which alternate between performances on stage and encounters offstage between the actors, John and Robert. In the course of these scenes the playwright has a good deal to say about the theater with a capital T and life with a small l, as well as other philosophical matters. He is preoccupied throughout with the energy of striving after relationships in the singular master-disciple form that attracts him.

The theatrical metaphor is an ancient one. All the world's a stage, even if some of us are merely stagehands. This has always been understood, since every life is a kind of experimental piece of acting. The theater is thus in everybody's blood. For example, Mamet's on-stage "play" scenes are dreary clichés, played comically as high camp: a World War I trenches drama; an "Elizabethan" play whose line of dialogue is as stale as last week's bread ("but *fly* my *liege* and *think* no *more* of *me*" 31); a "high" British comedy of manners (two ultracivilized men discussing the adultery one of them has committed with the wife of the other); a dreamy, romantic scene, probably meant to parody Chekhov; a single speech from a play about the French Revolution; a lifeboat scene from a sea play, perhaps, as Stephen Gale has suggested, an O'Neill play; a medical melodrama in the style of Sidney Kingsley or, as the scene turns out, Walter Mitty. Nevertheless, the use of these flawed scenes makes the point very well that more important than the quality of any particular drama is the very existence of theater. Ultimately the audience finds a way to respond, to laugh at the on-stage material and to become absorbed in the offstage. There is theater in both places, and Mamet plays with the forms of both.

But the best of Mamet's creations is a pair of shallow characters and a demonstration of how their frailty is of a piece with their calling in the theater. Robert the older and John the younger actor are just leaving the theater and have actually said good night to each other (so that the whole play may be taken as one big encore) when the following ensues:

> *ROBERT*: I thought the bedroom scene tonight was brilliant.
> *JOHN*: Did you?
> *ROBERT*: Yes, I did. (Pause.) Didn't you think it went well?
> *JOHN shrugs.*
> *ROBERT*: Well, I thought it went brilliantly.
> *JOHN*: Thank you.
> *ROBERT*: I wouldn't tell you if it wasn't so.
> *Pause.*
> *JOHN*: Thank you.
> *ROBERT*: Not at all. I wouldn't say it if it weren't so (1).

This is pure theatrical banality. The repetition of the actors' cliché words *brilliant* and *brilliantly*, the humble shrug and the thank-yous, the pretentious switch to the subjunctive mood ("if it weren't so") are all precisely observed by Mamet and carefully structured to produce an effect. Both in the reading and on stage the effect is to present a pair of predictably egotistical actors whose offstage role playing (here humble and sincere and freely giving praise) is as crucial to them and to the audience as their on-stage work. A life in the theater consists precisely in this duality.

The fun of this comedy lies in the abundance of such material and in the master-disciple structure through which it is woven. Thus Robert rarely neglects an opportunity to instruct John in everything from how to assure a safe fencing scene (keep the point of the weapon up) to achieving proper posture ("keep your back straight" 36) to acknowledgment of usable superstition ("please knock on wood" 31) to appropriate histrionic restraint ("Could you . . . perhaps . . . *do* less?" 41). In the beginning John is both eager to please the older man and a little naive about Robert's essentially conservative nature, so that he plays the disciple impeccably until things begin to change about halfway through the play.

In scene 13 John is visibly, though not verbally, bored with Robert's running commentary on the technique of the lifeboat-scene playwright. In scene 17, John's patience gives out and he is openly in opposition to his companion. Yet this is one of Mamet's most optimistic works, and almost as quickly as trouble flares between them, it is patched up. In response to Robert's pronunciamento that "On the boards, or in society at large. There must be law, there must be a reason, there must be tradition" (67), John apologizes for having told Robert to shut up, and though Robert declares he cannot be bought off so cheaply, he can and is. For as he has just noted, "What is 'life on stage' but attitudes? . . . Damn little." And John has found the proper attitude.

By scene 22 the relationship comes apart over John's good reviews. Robert's attitude has gone astray and John gains revenge by telling him to use his own towels. In the next scene, when Robert comes across John rehearsing alone in the empty theater and tries to make amends, John mocks him. The scene embodies the displacement of one generation by another. The action hangs on Robert's departure. Will he go or won't he? Will John be able to rehearse by himself or not? The text being rehearsed is a telling allusion: the lines are those spoken by the chorus at the outset of act 2 of Shakespeare's *Henry V*. But Henry V is Prince Hal of the *Henry IV* plays, a character whose destiny of displacing an older figure is realized in the later work and is the source of splendid dramatic and comedic action in the earlier. Besides, though the lines John is speaking ("Now all the youth of

DAVID MAMET

England are on fire / And silken dalliance in the wardrobe lies") invoke the passions of youth, the character who speaks them is a minor one in the Shakespeare play. Robert is moved enough by the displacement under way—John "following in the footsteps of . . . those who have gone before" (82)—to burst into tears and so provoke another conciliation. Nevertheless, Robert does not leave, and the scene ends with John's muttered "shit."

By scene 26, however, John is filled with compassion for Robert, and at the end there is a real camaraderie based on mutual feeling. Still, it is a life in the theater, and there are only "two *actors*" and "some *lines*." The ancient theater metaphor insists on the identity, and so does Robert ("the Theatre is, of course, a part of life" 81). Mamet's triumph is in mocking both on the same stage.

Glengarry Glen Ross (1984)

First produced in London in September, 1983, *Glengarry Glen Ross* was staged in February of 1984 at the Goodman Theatre in Chicago and moved to Broadway the same year. In New York it won the Pulitzer Prize for 1984. The play comes directly out of Mamet's experience as a high-pressure salesman hawking worthless land in Florida and Arizona over the telephone. The writer is at home with materials from his work life—witness *Lakeboat* and

A Life in the Theatre, for example—and has here produced a variation on the theme of the heartlessness of American business put on stage thirty-five years earlier by Arthur Miller in *Death of a Salesman* (1949).

The play continues its author's obsessive examination of competitive relations among men on the margins of legitimate business enterprise; in this sense it comes out of the same imaginative strand that produced *American Buffalo*. The vision here, however, is bleaker than in either *Salesman* or *Buffalo*. In *Salesman*, Biff had stolen a pen from a sales manager's office—not quite consciously—a mere hint of corruption peeking through the legitimacy of American business. In *American Buffalo* the setting as well as the business had deteriorated from an executive's office to a sleazy junk shop in a Chicago slum, and there is a robbery planned. There is dissension among the thieves and the burglary does not come off. In *Glengarry* there is also a plan to burglarize—this time an office—and the original plan also goes awry; but the burglary does come off, and the thief is apprehended. The corruption is thus seen to be complete, the so-called businessmen merely inept burglars.

The salesmen—Levene, Moss, and Aaronow—are described as "men in their fifties," in contrast to Williamson, the office manager, and

DAVID MAMET

Roma, the "star" of the sales force who are "men in their forties"—an oblique comment, perhaps, that it takes youth to get ahead in America. The older men are bitterly resentful that a sales contest is going on that gives them little chance to win. They must "close" deals to get on the "board" and be apportioned productive "leads," i.e., given the names of likely buyers. But without the productive leads they cannot get on the board, the customers they *do* close, old and unlikely leads, "kick out," or renege on the contracts they've signed. Only Roma is doing well; therefore, only he is given the prime leads. This pattern whereby the well-off continue to prosper and the less well-off continue to fail is thus seen to be built into the system.

At the outset Levene argues this point with Williamson. To try to get a few prime leads for himself he simply heaps calumny on Roma, whom he insists is not a "proven man," not a "closer"; but he does not persuade Williamson, and eventually he must make a deal to buy leads from the manager. However, he fails to produce the cash Williamson demands and gets only a couple of old leads. Moss and Aaronow, with similar attitudes and equally disgruntled, decide to break into the office, steal the good leads, and sell them to Jerry Graff, a former member of the sales force who has gone off to start his own thriving business—an exemplary American entrepreneur.

Act 1 ends with Aaronow's coerced agreement to the plan; he will be a partner to Moss, who has made the arrangements with Graff, and will do the actual breaking and entering. Act 2 finds the deed done and a detective on the premises investigating. Roma enters and flies into a rage until he is (falsely) assured that despite the disruptions of the theft his final sale to a man named Lingk has been registered and has made him the winner of the contest. Levene enters to report a huge sale to a pair of deadbeat clients, who turn out to be long-time "kick-outs." The surprise ending occurs when Williamson traps Levene into admitting that he, (not Aaronow), was the burglar—and Moss's partner in the enterprise.

Thus nothing is as it seems in *Glengarry Glen Ross*—only the pattern of coercion, aggression, corruption, and betrayal that Mamet sees underlying the efforts of these men striving to make a living in a heartless world.

The theatricality of the play depends on the intricate structure of this pattern of betrayal. For example, Mamet raises great expectations near the end of the second act when, as Levene is about to be arrested for burglary, Roma exhibits what looks like compassion for the older man. Roma declares

DAVID MAMET

that he and Levene are really friends: "We have to stick together" (105). But a moment later, when Levene is taken away by the detective, the greedy Roma is shouting at Williamson in betrayal of his new friend: "I GET HIS ACTION. . . . Whatever he gets for himself, I'm taking half" (107).

The same pattern is evident, among other places, in the second scene of act 1, when Moss traps Aaronow into his plan to rob the office. He does it by involving Aaronow, who "thought that we were only talking" (45), in a conspiratorial discussion:

> *AARONOW*: Why are you doing this to me, Dave. Why are you talking this way to me? I don't understand. Why are you doing this at all. . .?
> *MOSS*: That's none of your fucking business. . .
> *AARONOW*: Well, well, well. *talk* to me, we sat down to eat *dinner,* and here I'm a *criminal* . . . (45).

Thus is becomes clear that the aggressive hostility of Dave Moss is pervasive and mechanical. The answer to Aaronow's question—"Why are you doing this at all. . .?"—is given a moment later, as the scene ends:

> *MOSS*: I lied, [i.e., about how they would split the loot from the burglary]. . . In or out. You tell me, you're out you take the consequences.

AARONOW: I do?
MOSS: Yes. (Pause.)
AARONOW: And why is that?
MOSS: Because you listened (46).

Moss means that Aaronow happens to be part of this world. Whoever occupies that unfortunate position is likely to be caught in the net of corruption, willy-nilly, mechanically. When Levene argues with Williamson in the first scene of act 1, his case seems to be a reasonable one—that Mitch and Murry, who own the business, are rapacious for profits and that the business ethic they follow is the evil license by which an old and trusted employee, Levene, is tossed aside in order to whip the sales force into a competitive frenzy. Of course, this turns out to be wrong; things are much worse. Williamson is not mechanically enforcing corporate ethics; he's quite willing to be personally corrupt and sell Levene some leads; but then again Levene is as corrupt as he is.

The miracle of the play is that, even as we recoil from these men, who, when they are not corrupt, are, like Shelley Levene, filled with insupportable illusions, it enlists the audience's sympathy, at least for Levene and Aaronow. For ultimately there is something moving about the profoundly moral aspect of the striving—something deeply American—best expressed perhaps

DAVID MAMET

by Levene's "a man's his job" (94). In this respect *Glengarry Glen Ross* is linked to *Death of a Salesman*. Both are powerfully critical of the business of America, and both engage their audiences in the lives of those who sell.

Other Works

Mamet is a prolific writer. His canon so far consists of at least 28 plays, of which seven may be considered full-length. The following are the most significant and interesting of his other works.

The Water Engine is an interesting failure because it dramatizes Mamet's capacity to make something out of nothing, though winding up with too little. Written in 1976 as a radio play for the program *Earplay* on National Public Radio, the piece was first staged by the St. Nicks in Chicago on 11 May 1977 and subsequently in New York, first at the New York Shakespeare Festival in January, 1978, and then On Broadway at the Plymouth in March of the same year.

The play starts out to be a parody of a radio show and so thinks it had better parody the subject matter of the thirties—that is, that something about people was miraculous and they could do miraculous and simple things, like make a water engine; that something about capitalist economic institutions was intrinsically bad and capitalists would kill you for a buck. These ideas and a penchant for epic staging a la Brecht do the play in, however. For the work must carry a tremendous load of stagecraft—cinematic "cuts" between scenes, Chinese-opera manipulations of setting and props, radio control booth machinations with sound—to support a 1930s melodrama about a marvelous invention (the engine that runs on water) and whether big business America would murder the inventor and his sister in order to suppress the invention for economic reasons. The answer is that the pair are murdered. What the audience suspected comes about.

The relationship between this work and Mamet's major undertakings is slender. The theme of the murderousness of business is apparent, as are the interesting uses of theatricality and the engagement produced by theater. But there is neither the intensity in conception nor the interest in character that the other works feature, and *The Water Engine* tries hard to substitute a kind of poetic portentousness for these virtues (e.g., "Technological and ethical masterpieces decay into folk tales").

Reunion and *Dark Pony* (1979) are short, thematically related, two-character plays, each featur-

DAVID MAMET

ing a father and a daughter, focusing on the tender and movingly human moments in their lives and memories.

The Woods (1977) again examines the relations between the sexes but does so with the love that is absent from *Sexual Perversity in Chicago*. As a result this typically Mametian two-character dramatic exercise shows Mamet in a different light. His characters, Nick and Ruth, touched by this love—though to be sure the desperation of earlier work is still there—can be seen as children lost in the woods, huddling together for warmth, perhaps able to sustain a touching concern for each other till morning comes.

Mamet is one of the younger American playwrights and by all accounts filled with energy and confidence. The theater he has made is an incisive commentary on American life, gifted with hard-edged, street-corner humor and a subtext of striving after close and satisfying human relations. His playwright's imagination is informed by a mastery of theatricality and his commitment to the stage is notable enough to suggest that new phases in his development cannot be long in coming.

Notes

1. Quoted Bill Zehme, "Hot Chicago," *Vanity Fair* Nov. 1984: 54.

2. David Mamet, "Why I Write for Chicago Theater," *Vanity Fair* Nov. l984: 52-53.

3. Mamet 52-53.

4. Quoted Samuel G. Freedman, "The Gritty Eloquence of David Mamet," *New York Times Magazine* 21 Apr. 1985: 42,46.

5. Quoted Freedman 46.

6. Richard Christiansen, "The Young Lion of Chicago Theater," *Chicago Tribune Magazine* 11 July 1982: 11.

7. Quoted C. W. E. Bigsby, *A Critical Introduction to Twentieth-Century American Drama* (New York: Cambridge University Press 1985): 3: 261.

8. Page numbers in parentheses refer to the following editions: David Mamet, *Sexual Perversity in Chicago and Duck Variations* (New York: Grove, 1978); *American Buffalo* (New York: Samuel French, 1977); *A Life in the Theatre* Grove, 1978); *Glengarry Glen Ross* Grove, 1984).

9. Stephen H. Gale, "David Mamet: The Plays, 1972–1980," *Essays in Contemporary American Drama*, ed. Hedwig Bock and Albert Wertheim (Munich: Hueber, 1981) 207-33.

10. Richard Gottlieb, "The Engine That Drives Playwright David Mamett," *New York Times* 15 Jan. 1978: 2.1.

CHAPTER FIVE

"The People in This Play Are Black": *Ed Bullins*

Biography and Approaches to the Work

One of the most dynamic and disturbing figures on the American scene these last twenty years has lived a life close to the main currents of that troubled recent history. Although the arts section of the newspapers and various special publications were full of him from the late 1960s through the middle and late 70s, his name has quietly disappeared from public consciousness. The playwright in this chapter is black, and "the people in this play are Black" is a ritual beginning stage direction he insists on using. Most of his more than forty plays—and his two books of prose fiction—are out of print. Yet Ed Bullins must be counted as a formidable mover and maker of the American theater during this period under review.

Born in North Philadelphia on 2 July 1935, he went to his first school on the hard ground of Darien Street, where he lived with his mother ("I didn't know that much about my father")[1] in that ordinary black ghetto. Bullins, who early on joined a gang, recalls having to go through a rival gang's territory to get to junior high school: "That's how I lost my front teeth—one day, I was being wise with a cat and he just hit me in the mouth."[2] Bullins acquired all the experience necessary to hustle and survive in that environment. "I'm a street nigger," he has said; "I been on the streets most of my life, not only in Philly but in other cities. I'm a travelling man, a wanderer and a mover—here today, gone tomorrow."[3]

Bullins's travels began when he joined the navy at seventeen; but, contrary to his description of himself, they stopped in 1967, when he was put in touch with Robert Macbeth and the New Lafayette Theatre of Harlem and came to New York from California. In between, he had been a boxing champion on his navy ship in the Mediterranean, had come back to Philadelphia briefly and then headed West. There he attended, also briefly, Los Angeles City College and San Francisco State College, where he first began writing plays. Bullins's contacts with formal education were negative. He and college classes never mixed well, but the experience had the effect of confirming him in his superb sense of himself as a literary talent. His first play, *How Do You Do?* (1965), so impressed him that "I knew . . . this was my gift."[4] Bullins has

ED BULLINS

never ceased to believe in the size and splendor of this gift.

In the Bay area he was also for a time connected with the San Francisco Black House, a revolutionary political and cultural organization that he and Marvin X and Eldridge Cleaver and a group of their friends founded; at Black House, he became acquainted with the Black Panthers. Among the restless young blacks imbued with the 1960s fervor for radical change, Bullins gave vent to this penchant in himself. Eldridge Cleaver appointed him Minister of Culture of the Black Panther Party, and he thus became friendly with Bobby Seale and Huey Newton. But Bullins left the party in an ideological dispute; "culture is a gun" was not an aesthetic that he could live with. When more internal stresses broke up the Black House coalition of artists and political activists, Bullins tried to organize three or four black theater groups in the Bay area but with little success.

While on the West Coast, he had the good fortune to wander one night into a performance of *Dutchman* and *The Slave* by Imamu Amiri Baraka (then still known as LeRoi Jones). The history of art is filled with crucial, transforming experiences. And this was one of them. It enfranchised Bullins's material, the idiom of the angry black but beautiful ghetto that he was working in. Bullins was sure he was on the right track.

The track he had been on had led to the writing of, among other things, a group of one-acts, including *Dialect Determinism (or The Rally)*, *The Electronic Nigger*, and *Clara's Ole Man*. To get these produced was not easy. But among the three or four black theater groups Bullins founded was Black Arts/West, and among the projects undertaken by another group, the San Francisco Drama Circle, with the director Buck Hartman, was the production of Bullins's one-acts. They were performed, with indifferent success, wherever Bullins could get a hearing—in North Beach coffee houses and at San Francisco State College. Nothing daunted, Bullins was marking time when fate intervened.

In 1967 Bullins's New York agent showed Robert Macbeth a copy of *Goin' a Buffalo*. Macbeth was impressed enough to phone Bullins and then send him an airplane ticket for New York. Thus began nearly a decade's association with the New Lafayette, first as playwright-in-residence and subsequently as associate artistic director. In that period more than a third of Bullins's output was staged in Harlem under Macbeth's direction. This association both coincided with and stimulated a flowering of black theater in New York, and

ED BULLINS

Bullins's works were soon in demand at other theaters in that city. The New Lafayette had a short and brilliant life, stirring up Harlem audiences and creating a handsome body of work. It voted itself out of existence in 1974. While it lived, Bullins enjoyed the life of the controversial black playwright, propagandist, and resident intellectual and was quick to engage in a long dialogue on the inadequacy of white critics, the correct approach to black arts, and other subjects such as whether or not black actors ought to undertake Chekhov.

Perhaps the best publicized of his controversies was his disowning of the Lincoln Center production of his play *The Duplex* (see below, preceding the analysis of this play under Major Works). But Bullins managed to ruffle feathers elsewhere. The propagandist wrote open letters at the drop of a hat "to cause a play in the real world. They set a tone. They let people know where I'm coming from."[5]

In the late 60s and early 70s Bullins managed to keep writing at a characteristic rate. In addition to his plays—musicals with Mildred Kayden; the finishing of *We Righteous Bombers*, a play that had been begun by Kingsley B. Bass; and several brilliantly imagined children's plays on themes from black American history—he produced a collection of short prose pieces, *The Hungered One*

(1971), and a novel, *The Reluctant Rapist* (1973).
Moreover, he was editor of *Black Theatre*, a journal
published by the New Lafayette. In addition, he
wrote introductions to various play collections
and, finally, began to be employed as visiting
professor, teaching English and creative writing at
colleges and universities around the country.
Lately he has been conducting a workshop for new
playwrights and working in the press department
at the New York Shakespeare Festival.

Bullins was a shaker and mover in the creation
of the black theater of the 60s and 70s. Though
black theater had been a reality in America for 150
years, its special identity in the 60s rose from
sentiments such as these of Langston Hughes:

> But someday somebody'll
> Stand up and talk about me,
> And write about me—
> Black and beautiful—
> And sing about me,
> And put on plays about me!
> I reckon it'll be
> Me Myself!
> Yes, it'll be me.

In 1965 Amiri Baraka demanded a theater *about*
black people, *with* black people, *for* black people,

ED BULLINS

and *only* black people.[6] To this demand there was a significant response all across the country. But "the movement is not one of solidarity in which all the people do one thing."[7] The New Lafayette Theater of Robert Macbeth and Ed Bullins forbade white critics to attend. In fact, they produced not just plays but rituals that were designed to pull a black audience together in racial and aesthetic solidarity. "Consciously," Bullins noted in 1971, "I attempt to exclude as many European and Western references as possible."[8] Not every black theater company of the period had such astringent purity of motives toward white audiences, critics, and dramatic theory and practice.

Nevertheless, the aim of black theater was to appeal directly to black audiences to the exclusion of whites. The idea was that the brutality of the black experience in America demanded a separate aesthetic response from its artists. No white could understand or appreciate what had to be done. The task was to show black audiences authentic images of themselves. And though there are differences of opinion about the identity of "themselves," for most of the black writers working in the theater it would be the poorest, most oppressed classes of the urban ghettos. As J. E. Gaines, another writer associated with the New Lafayette, put it, "What I write about are my experiences with Black people . . . in Harlem bars, pool rooms, theaters and basements. I go into basements that I know. I grew up in a basement. I go where niggers go."[9] Unlike the ideological, revolutionary theater of Amiri Baraka, which aimed at shaking its audience into agit/prop actions, the New Lafayette which nurtured Bullins believed that its job was to "show black people who they are, where they are, and what condition they are in."[10] The effect of this representation was to confer a new prestige on a black audience. It has had the further healing effect on the community that Macbeth has said is vital to the New Lafayette enterprise.

One of the elements of the style of black art, Macbeth has said, is that in it "black people can signify to one another without language."[11] Some of the obvious elements that make up the alphabet of the "secret language used in Black theater," according to Bullins himself, are

naturally, rhythm—black, blues, African; the racial consciousness and subconsciousness of Third World peoples; Black Cultural Nationalism, Black Revolutionary Nationalism and traditional Black people's familial nationalism; dance, as in Black life style and patterns; Black religion in its numerous forms—gospel, negro spiritualism to African spirit, sun, moon, stars and ancestor worship; Black astrology, numerology and symbolism; Black mysticism, magic and myth-science; also history, fable and legend, vodun ritual-ceremony,

ED BULLINS

Afro-American nigger street styles, and, of course, Black music.[12]

These loosely stated theoretical ideas are the background against which to see Bullins. They explain, for example, the care and affection and artistry with which Bullins places on stage a whole nation of ghetto characters, sharply drawn, distinct, filled with vitality and human dimension. They illuminate what he does with dance, music, and "Afro-American nigger street styles." They sponsor what has been criticized as his naturalism.[13] They account for the dignity and affection invested in his depictions of street culture.

Bullins's drama goes unflinchingly into the dreams and drives of the black culture, its special forms of language, music, dance, and interpersonal relations. Bullins is the great black dramatist of sexual relations; his work gives a precise picture of how black men and women relate and leaves to its audience the proper response to such visions. He is, moreover, a humorist in a rich American vein—the writer who sees humor arising from the vagaries of character. Bullins's people are continually striving, rarely achieving what they set out to do. But they are strikingly, soberly, there. They are objects of modernist consciousness—fit "presences" for contemplation in new American theater—phenomena caught with an artist's instrument.

Major Works

Goin' a Buffalo (1968)

The play, subtitled a Tragifantasy, is the work that Bullins's New York agent showed to Robert Macbeth that led to Bullins's association with the New Lafayette. However, it was given its first production, two staged readings, at the American Place Theatre in New York on 6 and 7 June 1968, under the direction of Roscoe Orman. It was subsequently produced by the New Lafayette and elsewhere. Though it is not one of Bullins's cycle plays, the structural plan of the play—entertaining the dream of a journey to the Promised Land—anticipates a structural idea present in *In the Wine Time* and *In New England Winter*.

The tragedy is in the way the dream is realized, in betrayal and ruthlessness.[14] The fantasy consists of the quality of the dream itself, which has little basis in reality. Moreover, fantasy aptly characterizes the means of representation that Bullins employs: light changes, color wheels, on-stage and offstage music, notably the jazz idioms of Max Roach, Clifford Brown, and Miles Davis, mingling with opportunistic frozen tableaux, characters placed in unmoving gestural relation to one another for special dramatic emphases, and one fleeting flashback to the first meeting of Curt and Pandora.

The journey from warm Los Angeles, where the action takes place in the early 1960s, to frozen Buffalo seems like a movement from life to death. But Buffalo is made to share with other literary and, especially, biblical destinations the ineffable quality of the sacred and the talismanic. "I heard that Buffalo is really boss" (83).[15] Thus what holds our attention about the dream is not whether it is sensible or not, but rather that these people, like a biblical tribe, are bound together in hopes of the magical change such journeys are thought to bring about. Curt, Rich, Shaky, Pandora, and Mamma-Too-Tight are thieves, whores, junkies, murderers, and pimps, but as outcast blacks in the deeps of the Los Angeles ghetto they share with the Israelites in Egypt a condition of slavery and a yearning to be free. Though Bullins is essentially a moralist, he does not condemn them for their transgressions but rather links them to a common motif in the human search for remission of suffering.

The central action of act 1 is the initiation of Art into the tribe. Art can become a member because he shares with the others certain characteristics of the black street hustler. His instinctive class solidarity accounts for his having rescued Curt in the jail riot; he is profoundly needy, arriving hungry at the door of Curt and Pandora's apartment; he has a murder on his rap sheet, has been a wanderer in foreign lands and been enmeshed in the culture of drugs. Most important, he has known betrayal. His story of his betrayal by a narc, winding up with "puke" and marijuana ground under his shoes, is a ritual confession that precedes his reintroduction to smoke through the medium of Pandora's seductive urgings. Once he has taken a few drags, and has been made to touch the other thing hidden in her box, the nickel-plated revolver, he is included. "Buffalo's goin'a be a gas" (44), says Pandora, and at the curtain, Art says that his car can get them as far as Buffalo.

The plan to go to Buffalo is, however, a fragile one, depending literally on their scraping together every penny they can. Curt needs some "grand theft dough" to make restitution for bad checks he has passed and for "juice" to use as bribes to get a pending case against him dismissed (31). In the second act, in the hallucinatory atmosphere of the nightclub where Pandora works as a stripper, the plan begins to unravel in disappointment and violence.

In act 3 Art perpetrates his betrayal and orders

ED BULLINS

the women to pack. When Pandora asks where they are going—when it becomes finally clear that he intends to leave Shaky, Curt, and Rich in jail—the answer he gives is "To Buffalo, baby, where else?" (97).

In the course of showing how the dream is destroyed, Bullins dramatizes in detail the complex codes of loyalty by which the group lives. These codes include the rules governing male/female relations. The group is bound together by the imperatives of male-sanctioned conduct. People accept their places in the scheme of things according to these rules. As these work in the pimp/whore relationship, for example, when Shaky says to Mamma, "A hundred stone cold dollars, baby. Tonight, baby!" her response must be exactly the prideful one she gives: "How do you want them, daddy . . . in fives or tens?" (23). Shaky's status depends on his speedily providing bail for Mamma. Curt would do the same for Pandora. And after the melee at the end of act 2, when Shaky has been picked up at the club with a stash of drugs, it is automatically understood that before the group can leave for Buffalo, Shaky must be bought free of jail. Art must be cared for when he arrives early in act 1 because loyalty is reciprocal, and when Art twice intervenes to prevent a man's striking his woman, it is clear that he must apologize. Because everyone is caught up in showing loyalty to Art when he tells his story, nobody sees the exact significance of his treacherously shooting the husband of his lover.

Females, on the other hand, are entirely responsible to the males. They have no autonomy and must do as they are told—although the roles seem to suit them and they express little resentment about them. Not that they don't see the inequality: Pandora notices that it's beans for Mamma her first night on the streets but chicken for Art when he comes to visit. But what she or Mamma manage to see amounts to nothing since they do not act on it.

Moreover, the women are exploited the way ordinary property is exploited. Shaky "owns" Mamma-Too-Tight, just as if she were a black woman, and though Curt and Pandora are married, Curt owns her. Rich would like to "take over" Mamma when Shaky is arrested but is prevented from doing so by Mamma's (and Curt's) belief that Shaky's rights are protected: he will be bailed out and resume property rights over Mamma. Women are thus sought after as sources of income, as the nightclub owner Deeny, according to Curt, seeks to gain control over Pandora and the other show girls to turn them out and enlarge his "stable." Or they are stolen—as a thief might steal an ordinary valuable—as Art steals them in his great betrayal. James Hatch is surely wrong in describing Art as a figure of the "baad dude" black character inherited from nineteenth-century black drama.[16] There is neither fun nor bravura display nor rebelliousness in him; instead he is a piece of pure treachery; ironically, his blackness, his membership in the tribe—in fact everything we see him standing for—directs the audience and the other characters to believe in his innate decency.

The dream in *Goin' a Buffalo* ends more bitterly than its biblical parallel. The original dreamer is not even in sight of the Promised Land, while the others start their journey in chains.

In the Wine Time (1968)

American dramatists since O'Neill have been peculiarly drawn to the dramatic cycle. In the last twenty years alone Wilson, Shepard, and Bullins have produced such cycles. It is perhaps a response to the largeness of our experience, though it is certainly a traditional form from the Greeks through the medieval drama of Western Europe. *In the Wine Time* is the first play in what Bullins calls the twentieth-century cycle. More ambitious than the undertakings of either O'Neill, Wilson, or Shepard, Bullins's epic conception aims at nothing less than to "chronicle a sense of the century for black people—examine all the major issues, the heart of the problems they face, their identity crises, economic and social movement, their mating, wedding and bedding."[17] To date, six plays in the cycle have emerged; in addition to this one, they are #2, *In New England Winter*, #3 *The Duplex*, #4 *The Fabulous Miss Marie*, #5 *Home Boy*, and #6 *Daddy*. Either Cliff Dawson or Steve Benson or both appear in the first four plays. Through the sensibility of these two, attention is directed to the worlds the plays inhabit.

In the Wine Time opened at the New Lafayette Theatre on 10 December 1968 under the direction of Robert Macbeth. The play begins with a prologue spoken by sixteen-year-old Ray. In it he describes a piercingly sweet but wordless attraction he had conceived during a nostalgic summer long ago for a beautiful, airy-light girl. The terms of his description raise her to the level of an archetypal figure, and one day the girl speaks. She must go away but tells him, "I'll be waiting. All you'll need to do is search!" (105). This lyrical prologue introduces a major structural motif of Bullins's work, the search. It also offers sharp and ironic contrast with what follows. The girl shows up in the play and becomes a kind of bitterly disappointing talisman for Ray: a beautiful promise but a hope unfulfilled. Moreover, the hope and the

ED BULLINS

promise she holds out are echoed in the heartfelt slogans that Cliff Dawson flings at the boy: "It's your world, son" (129) and "It's your world, Ray . . . Go on out there and claim it" (182). Liz in *In New England Winter* is a similarly beckoning figure.

The action of the play proper takes place on a ghetto side street, Derby Street, in the heat of summer, "in the early 1950's" (107). It is evening, the wine time. The street is heavily peopled, and the inhabitants act out a seemingly aimless Chekhovian opening moment. The only white residents, the Krumps, are trying to get the soused Mr. Krump up the stairs from where he stands, wrapped around a street lamp. There is shouting and uncertain movement. Bama and Red, two menacing figures, advance. Cliff and Ray and Lou, not yet seen as leading characters, drink wine. Cliff uses foul language. Ray goes to help Krump. Miss Minny urges him on. Cliff says no. Bunny comes on unnoticed, though Ray will say later, "Me and her's in love" (147). Ray carries Krump upstairs and gets a boot in the pants from Red as he does so. And another moment begins. In Chekhov the point is that a calm aimlessness reveals everything. In Bullins the lack of calm is also aimless, also revealing.

Thus another element of Bullins's craft is the

subtle interpenetration and linking of moments. Ghetto life, his dramatic form seems to say, is composed of such moments. Within them the raw emotional lives of the residents are melodically stated and varied. They are blues and jazz riffs, broken off with suddenness and impact some-times, sometimes swelling to big-wave heights like the irresistible swell of gospel choruses. Within them, in any case, these internal forces pitch emo-tions to heights and depths along an inevitably rising curve.

The tune of one of these emotional lines is carried by Cliff and his discontents. Currently a student because he wants to improve his lot in life, Cliff is a former navy man who spent most of his enlistment in the brig. Angry, witty, a drunk and an outcast, Cliff has character and recognizes it in others (like Lou) when he sees it. He is determined not to be an animal, one of the "Derby Street Donkeys" (130) among whom he despises living.

> CLIFF: I'm goin' ta get me part of that world or stare your God in the eye and scream why. I am not a beast . . . an animal to be used for the plows of the world. But if I am then I'll act like one, I'll be one and turn this . . . world of dreams and lies and fairy tales into a jungle or a desert. . . . There's a world out there, woman. Just beyond that lamppost

ED BULLINS

. . . just across "The Avenue" and it'll be mine and Ray's (139).

The balance of act 1 is taken up with the long moment of Cliff's agony and the parallel story of Ray's wish to get out of the life that Cliff is describing by securing Lou's permission to join the navy. As the wine time grows longer in the night, Cliff speaks of his condition directly, but it is also dramatized. As he screams at and strikes Lou, his conflicted suffering is apparent. Ray must get "off'a Derby Street and away from here so he can grow up to be his own man."

> LOU (*Crying*): Like you?
> CLIFF: No, not like me . . . not tied down to a half-grown, scared, childish bitch!
> LOU: You don't have to be.
> CLIFF: But I love you. (135–136)

Though Cliff knows Ray must go, he also knows that as long as both remain on Derby Street, only Derby Street values can prevail. Cliff is helpless to teach Ray what to do in the interim. Ray can only follow Cliff's lead and keep up with his consumption of wine. He can only see Cliff beating up the pregnant Lou and be told to emulate it. If Bunny gives him trouble, "you knock her on her ass, ya hear?" (162). Nevertheless, it is not true that, as Lou says, "The only thing wrong with Ray is you,

Cliff'' (160). What's wrong with Ray is the soil in which both he and Cliff are withering.

By the end of act 2 Cliff and Ray have gone off with Silly Willy Clark, who has the cash to buy them a "big man" of wine. Lou thinks that they're "probably out lookin' for some ole funky bitches" (167) as well. Bama, Red, Tiny, Bunny, and Doris occupy the stoop of the Dawson's house when, at the beginning of act 3, Lou makes this observation. It soon becomes an irony when Doris reveals that Cliff has had sexual relations with Tiny. Tempers become frayed and knives come flashing out. The fatal violence that ensues does not resolve but rather ends the play as Cliff disarms and then stabs Red to death. At last the cop on the beat, whom Cliff had earlier disdained because the officer called him "Cliff," shows some respect: "I have to warn you, Mr. Dawson . . . ," to which Cliff replies with a genuine, "Yes, sir" (181).

As Cliff is led away in handcuffs, he urges Ray for the last time to take hold of the world: "Go on out there and claim it" (182). But this is no romance, and the play does not end there. The audience cannot be left with a glimmer of hope. Instead, Bullins uses a telling little four-speech coda to make a powerful point: that though something awful has happened tonight, things will probably be no different tomorrow. The ordinary horror of ghetto experience will be discussed over tea the next day.

> *MISS MINNY*: Come down for tea, Beatrice, dear, and I'll tell you all about it.
> *BEATRICE*: All right, Miss Minny. The Lord bless you tonight.
> *MISS MINNY*: He will, dear . . . 'cause he works in mysterious ways.
> *BEATRICE (starting off)*: Amen! (182).

In New England Winter (1971)

The second play in the twentieth-century cycle was given its first performance by Woodie King, Jr.'s New Federal Theater in February of 1971. Although the character of Steve Benson is not new to the Bullins oeuvre, this is his first appearance in the cycle. The play alternates its seven scenes between the years 1955 and 1960. The action of 1960 consists of the planning and execution of a robbery to be pulled off by Steve, his half brother Cliff Dawson, and their two accomplices, Chuckie and Bummie. The scenes set in 1955 take place at the home shared by Liz—Steve's obsession—and her sister Carrie. At Liz's place there are also Liz' husband, Oscar, and his wretched sidekick, Crook (a character of that name made a small and equally sinister appearance in *The Duplex*). The dream

journey motif—toward Liz and New England winter—dominates the action in 1960.

The prologue is a lyrical encapsulation in
prose of the dramatic action of the play. It alternates between a narrator's memory (presumably
Steve's) of the robbers going off to pull the job and
his recollections of ecstatic moments with a woman
(presumably Liz). Like the prologue of *In the Wine
Time* this one holds out the promise of a "world out
there," in the metaphor of the unnamed woman,
and in Steve's inner reply to Cliff's question about
whether he has any plans now that the robbery has
taken place and the swag divided:

Two very simple ones: pray for winter and head north
(133).

Once again, there is promise; again it is in the
context of frozen weather.

As the play opens in Cliff's room, somewhere
in California in 1960, Steve is reminiscing about Liz
in the same frozen terms:

I think about her all the time. (*Reminiscing.*) It's snowing up there now. Snowing . . . Big white flakes.
Snow. Silent like death must be (137).

These are the terms, moreover, in which Liz thinks
of him: Steve is "wild like only a northern nigger

can be wild. All of it inside, mostly, and cold and sharp and slick like ice" (149).

We learn that Cliff has done his time for killing Red in *In the Wine Time*, and that he is filled with a raging bitterness because his wife, Lou, has disappeared with his son and another child she has had by an unknown man. He wants revenge against the transgressor. He is also bitter at Steve because Steve had been living with Lou and knew the man but will not give Cliff his name. Steve protects the secret by killing Bummie before he can reveal it. But the ironic twist in this plot is that Cliff had known the name all along: it was Steve.

Steve Benson is a different character here than the one in the earlier play. The others call him "Professor" and allude to his bookishness, but here his character is more rigidly controlled. He seems more desperate. He insists on interminable practice for the robbery. In charge of the caper, he is devoted to the disciplined use of the intellect. It is a devotion with which he hopes to "get myself ready to meet the future" (160). For when all is said and done, chaos rules his inner life. When Liz goes mad in scene 6, he insists:

It can't be this way. This isn't it. . . . there must be order . . . perfection . . . there must be form . . . there must be reason and absolutes . . .There can't be only madness and reaching out and never touching the sides (167).

But Steve cannot turn the tide of madness in which he is being drowned.

The conflict between Steve and Cliff goes deep and is at the heart of the play. For example, opposed to Steve's rigid conception of how the robbery should be prepared is Cliff's disdain for details and disciplined preparation: "All we got to do is get up off our asses and walk in there and take what we want" (158). Cliff has a typical womanizer's attitude toward women, while Steve's is the attitude of a radical romantic who sees his passion as an ecstatic opportunity to establish an ideal relationship with Liz. Cliff understands that nothing changes. Steve does not, and the play's major ironies are generated around this dream of Steve's.

But Liz, whom he has idealized, is not in her right mind. Though Steve is a desperate navy deserter hiding out in her bed, Liz angrily denies he is a wino. Her idealizations are on a par with his: "The night's our home," she says. "We're children of the black god of night" (150). She wants only to have his child and to range across the country with it, from the Pacific to Florida, in some kind of mythicizing baptism of a mad American

ED BULLINS

dream. "I'm his queen!" she exults. But when Steve wakes, he is merely a wino. And when he is discovered innocently sleeping it off wrapped in Carrie's arms, Oscar exacts revenge by sending for the shore patrol. Liz goes entirely mad, and Steve flees into the night, with the warped and evil Crook waiting in the wings to possess Liz, passing himself off as Steve.

Liz's poetically desperate need to bear Steve's child is reminiscent of Velma's similar need in *The Duplex*. Here we are meant to see that need against, for example, Oscar's memories of a childhood in which his father spoke only to tell him to get out of the way and Crook's thwarted attempt to rape Carrie when she was eleven. Bullins's views of such matters are balanced by irony. For Steve is to be displaced here by Crook as he is in *The Duplex* by O.D.

The final scene is pure irony, for it takes place in 1960, after Steve has fled from the shore patrol. The scene ends with the death of Bummie and Chuckie's stark curtain line as he begins to wrap the body in a sheet: "I knew him . . . I knew him" (174). Steve still needs "travelin' money." For he still intends to "pray for winter 'n head north." Once again the dream has turned to ashes. Once again a spark remains lit.

UNDERSTANDING CONTEMPORARY DRAMA

The Duplex: A Black Love Fable in Four Movements (1972)

The premiere performance of *The Duplex* took place at the New Lafayette Theatre in May of 1970, but its subsequent production by the Repertory Theatre of Lincoln Center, under the direction of Gilbert Moses, was the one that caused the trouble. Fifteen days before the play was scheduled to open on 9 March 1972, Bullins began issuing a series of denunciations of the production and demanding that it be canceled.[18] The playwright claimed that "the original black intentions of the work" had been subverted and that the "artistic assassins" into whose hands he had entrusted his play had turned it into "another darkie minstrel show."[19] "What they [the Lincoln Center administrators, curiously enough, not the director Gilbert Moses] really want to do is sell to White people a negative image of Blacks and bestial types fornicating all over the stage, acting like lustful clowns."[20] The critics, at least one of whom was embarrassed to review a work that the author had denounced, were divided. Some thought it among his best, while others, notably Walter Kerr, thought it without coherent form or dramatic resolution.[21] Kerr, however, seems wrong.

The structural pattern of the play is clear and

ED BULLINS

formal enough. The short school holiday of Steve Benson is the time frame of the action. Another, perhaps more important, framing device is provided by the early focus on the lively bad dude, Montgomery Henderson, and his final appearance, articulating in his vital little speech that the frustrating round of events of the drama is soon to be repeated. This is a characteristic Bullins strategy, useful and effective.

The desultory, sexy, comic, drunken, violent, and ultimately telling movements are separated by interludes of song—blues, jazz, and scat numbers that set mood and tome for the groups of scenes they precede. At the end of the first movement Steve and Velma are making love and Velma is begging Steve, "You gotta be my man, now, Stevie. Now you gotta!" (49). By the end of the second movement Steve is about to make love to Marie Horton, while downstairs O.D is brutally taking Velma. To make love to Marie he must ignore Velma's crying out his name for help. At the end of the third movement Steve is nearly killed by a friend of O.D.'s who sneaks into his room with a knife. Moments before the final curtain Steve finally attacks O.D. and is himself nearly strangled to death.

There is no resolution in all this in the sense that an Ibsen play resolves itself, through crafted, articulated plot developments. Rather the resolution here is a poetic one, an image doing the work of articulated development. It is precisely Bullins's point—perhaps an important point of his whole oeuvre—that in the black experience images may arrest a particular moment in an artist's visionary flux, but there are no resolutions. The business of life in the black ghetto is not yet organized for such resolution.

The play begins with the riotous pinochle game and introduces the male occupations in Velma's duplex—jiving horseplay; playing with language, mainly obscenities; sparring over cards (as with the chess game in *Goin' a Buffalo*); discussing women and sex; concentrating on booze, marijuana, and pleasure in general. There is an admirable intimacy in this. Montgomery's mock threat to sexually assault his son Marco is a measure of the freedom of the interplay. (A reader of the play does not see the "lustful clowns" that Bullins's saw in Moses's production.) The card game that continues throughout keeps dramatizing this male interplay.

Bullins's central preoccupation with male/female relations is at the heart of the play. These relations are worked out principally with the central characters: Velma, who owns the duplex with her husband, O.D., and Steve Benson. In reading

ED BULLINS

Velma a piece of the prologue of *In the Wine Time*, Benson may be ambiguously identified as a figure of the author. Steve Benson is, in any case, the sensibility through which Bullins has filtered much of the cycle. He appears in *In the Wine Time*, *The Fabulous Miss Marie*, and *It Has No Choice* (a noncycle play) as well as in several early prose pieces. Steve, like Bullins in his California days, is a student and, if he is the author of what he reads aloud, also a poet. Caught between his ambition and his inability to separate himself from the milieu of the duplex, he is left with giving in to his impulses. When the play opens, he has already begun an affair with the married Velma. Later on he will sleep with Marie.

The whole subject is introduced in scene 1 of the first movement, when Tootsie describes his relationship to Lola. He and Lola have been broken up for three years.

We ain't never been together 'cept'n fo' two months when we first got married. But her mother was livin' wit us den, so I got in a couple of hassles wit Lola and her mamma and then I split. I still go back and see her. We good friends (14).

Still married, Tootsie takes good care of her. For though he knows that not all of Lola's children are his, "dey might as well be mine," because "kids need somebody fo' dere fatha" (13-14). Tootsie's relations to Lola are made more complex by his particular rule of sexual possessiveness: since he and Marco are friends, he would kill Marco if he were to catch him with her. On the other hand, he says, it does not matter to him if the other man is a stranger. Later on Marco tells another story about Tootsie and Lola that subverts this rule: Tootsie punches out a stranger who has been making a pass at Lola in public. The other men tease him about Lola, but they can also envy the woman he loves. As Marco puts it, "Many's the day I've wished I was a bitch and Tootsie Franklin was in love with me" (81). In the world of *The Duplex* the relationship between Tootsie and Lola and the one between the ancient drunken couple, Mamma and Pops, are the standards by which to judge all.

Although Mamma and Pops (whose name is revealed to be Clifton Slaughter Dawson, the long-lost father of Cliff Dawson of *In the Wine Time* and *In New England Winter*) seem to wander crazily through the play, Bullins makes them out to be models of how men and women may relate. They are loving and loyal to each other throughout, and Mamma's moving speech about Pops's life, near the end of the third movement, reveals an exchange of intimacies that solidifies their bonds.

By these standards O.D. is clearly a beast

ED BULLINS

outside the pale of civilization. His behavior toward Velma sets in motion Steve's better impulses. Steve comforts Velma when O.D. slashes her and tries to protect Velma from him at the end. O.D., however, is almost a cartoon, a poster figure, present in the play as a kind of monstrous projection of the depths of the human condition. Velma knows that O.D is impossible, but she is searching for something more stable than either O.D. or the vacillating Steve. Thus she makes an effort to have human relations with O.D.—only to be stabbed for her troubles.

By these same standards Steve can be found wanting in the absolute sense. But he is conflicted. On the one hand he, like O.D., wants nothing from Velma but sex—when and where he wants it. As they are making love on the floor, where he has pushed her down at the end of the first movement, when Velma asks him to be her man, all he can say is, "Yeah, I know, baby. I know" (49). When Velma tells him she is pregnant, his response is, "Let's talk about it later" (111)—a conversation that never takes place. Yet he is filled with tenderness for her. In the third movement he declares "I love her!" (118) and he plans "to get her." His long speech at the end of scene 2 of the third movement may contain some gratuitous rhetoric ("But where the hell are we going, brother? Where? Into the machine maze of I.B.M."), but it also strikes deep chords of genuine feeling:

> Nobody knows the love and beauty I feel in holding my woman in my arms . . . a poor little scared black girl that's even dumber than I'm supposed to be. . . . (121-122).

Although Bullins has noted that he consciously tried to eliminate European and Western references from his work, he has nevertheless taken a good deal of the dramatic form of these plays from Chekhov. Some of the sixteen scenes in the play are violent little melodramas—such as O.D.'s robbery of Velma's savings, Crook's foiled attempt to either cut or kill Steve, and the final savagery between Steve and O.D. Some, like scene 2 of the first movement, are almost pure exposition. Most, however, are in the Chekhovian mood of a desultory unfolding of character, longing, and unfulfilled wish. Even the long party sequences of the second movement, inaugurated by the arrival of Marie Horton and her niece Wanda, fall into this category. In these there is a strain of metaphysical lament.[22] The mood mourns an absurdity that is cosmic.

For in the midst of the turmoil of wine, sex, drugs, and violence there is a powerful sense of the angst of the human condition here. The inhabitants of the black California scene that Bullins depicts, sharply drawn as characters, are engaged in a struggle to live against the currents of what would drown them. And live they do, with considerable vitality. Racism is barely mentioned in the play, but in this authentic staging of the black dilemma Bullins has created powerful and shapely theater.

Other Works

There is some truth to the critical view that Bullins's entire canon is more impressive in the aggregate than any single play. In the canon, however, there are sketchy agit/prop pieces like *The American Flag Ritual*, in which a character relieves himself on the American flag and wipes his feet on it. There are didactic works like *Dialect Determinism* and anti-white audience plays like *It Bees Dat Way*. Bullins has written musicals such as *Sepia Star* and *Storyville* and *House Party* that do not come from his deepest sources of inspiration. But he has also written individual short works of distinction like *Clara's Ole Man*, a work of extraordinary power and subtlety: in our dramatic literature, there is hardly a more moving or unsparing portrait of the bitter irony in our streets. Bullins has also written two highly imaginative historical works for children, *I am Lucy Terry* and *The Mystery of Phyllis Wheatley*. That they are not performed more frequently impoverishes our theater.

Although *The Fabulous Miss Marie* adds strongly to the Cycle, the last two Cycle plays, *Home Boy* and *Daddy*, are not so strong. Nevertheless, Bullins's work as a whole has accomplished what he, in conjunction with the New Lafayette, had planned and hoped to do, that is, to show black people an image of themselves they could live with. Bullins is an artist of considerable power, and the impulse to continue his project is unlikely to have been extinguished entirely. More of his work would be welcome. It would, as in the past, add to the light on American stages.

Notes

1. Jervis Anderson, "Profiles: Dramatist," *New Yorker* 16 June 1973: 44. Anderson is the principal source for information on Bullins's life. He is supplemented by documents in the Hatch-Billops Collection.

2. Anderson 46.

3. Anderson 46.

4. Anderson 48.

5. Mel Gussow, "Bullins, the Artist and the Activist, Speaks," *New York Times* 22 Sept. 1971: 44.

6. Baraka is paraphrased in James V. Hatch, "A White Folks

ED BULLINS

Guide to 200 Years of Black & White Drama," *The Drama Review* 16: 4 (1972): 18.

  7. Erika Munk, "Up from Politics: An Interview with Ed Bullins," *Performance* #2 (Apr. 1972): 54.

  8. Gussow 44.

  9. Ed Bullins, ed., *The New Lafayette Theatre Presents* (Garden City, NY: Anchor, 1974): 70.

  10. Robert Macbeth, quoted Anderson 62.

  11. Anderson 62.

  12. Ed Bullins, *The Theme Is Blackness: The Corner and Other Plays* (New York: Morrow, 1973) 9.

  13. C. W. E. Bigsby, *A Critical Introduction to Twentieth-Century American Drama* (New York: Cambridge University Press, 1985): 3:408.

  14. Ruby Cohn, *New American Dramatists: 1960–1980* (New York: Grove, 1982) 105.

  15. Page numbers in parentheses refer to the following editions: *Goin' a Buffalo* and *In the Wine Time*, in *Five Plays by Ed Bullins* (Indianapolis: Bobbs-Merrill, 1969); *The Duplex: A Black Love Fable in Four Movements* (New York: Morrow, 1971); *In New England Winter*, *New Plays from the Black Theatre*, ed. Ed Bullins (New York: Bantam, 1969).

  16. Hatch 11.

  17. Brandon R. Blackman IV, "Black Hope of Broadway," *Sepia* 24 1975): 67.

  18. According to the standard Dramatists' Guild contract in force at the time, Bullins had the power to stop the production.

  19. Anderson 41.

  20. Clayton Riley, "Bullins: 'It's Not the Play I Wrote,'" *New York Times* 12 Mar. 1972: 1.7.

  21. Walter Kerr, "Mr. Bullins Is Himself at Fault," *New York Times* 19 Mar. 1972: 1.

  22. Bigsby 406.

CHAPTER SIX

Down and Out in Lebanon and New York:
Lanford Wilson

Biography and Approaches to the Work

Like no other recent American playwright Lanford Wilson has been intimately associated with a theater group for an extended period of time—in his case, more than fifteen years. He is one of the founders of the Circle Repertory Company and its resident playwright. Since 1969 the company has done most of his plays, and several of these have been written with specific actor-members in mind. The effect of this on his craftsmanship has been salutary. Before 1969 he was closely connected with both Caffe Cino, where his first play (*So Long at the Fair*) was performed, and Cafe La Mama, a haven for Lower East Side writers of the early 60s. Wilson was not just a writer but also an actor and designer at those theaters; his theatrical acumen helped shape his career, limiting the compass of his work to small spaces

LANFORD WILSON

and forcing his ingenuity toward high invention.

Wilson was born in Lebanon, Missouri, the site of the Talley plays, on 13 April 1937. When he was five, his parents divorced. His father moved to California and found work in the aircraft industry, while his mother took him to Springfield, Missouri. From there he moved with her to Ozark when, some six years later, she married a farmer. After graduating from high school in Ozark and spending a year at Southwest Missouri State College, he moved to San Diego to be near his father. But as is hinted in the autobiographical *Lemon Sky*, the reunion was not a success. Wilson got on well enough with his stepmother and stepbrothers but not with his father.

After a year in California, spending his time variously as an aircraft worker and attending San Diego State College—where he first began to write plays—Wilson came east to Chicago, where he stayed nearly six years. Chicago energized him. A desultory writing habit took hold, and he began to complete and send out short stories while earning his keep as an advertising copywriter. Still restless, the playwright came to New York late in 1962 and almost immediately made connections at Caffe Cino and Cafe La Mama. Wilson's first play was performed at Caffe Cino in August of 1963, and his work has rarely been off the boards for very long since then.

A meticulous craftsman, Wilson has experimented with expressionistic devices and highly theatrical effects—all for the purpose of creating a theater of intense effect. He has experimented with impressionism, with works for voices, and with abstract plays for acrobatic performers. His realism is authentic but never without a hint of mockery, as if taking the form to task for its pieties. In his more than thirty plays he has undertaken to put on stage a kind of epic encompassment of American experience and mythologies. His characters "work" on stage; the narratives they operate in have a driving force that holds the interest of his audiences. Moreover, he is capable of putting on stage whole communities, as in the plays of the trilogy, *The Rimers of Eldritch*, *Hot l Baltimore*, and *Balm in Gilead*. He has also undertaken the exploration of individual psychology, such as in *The Madness of Lady Bright*.

One of Wilson's central interests is the powerless, the outcast, and the downtrodden. He sees them living in transient uncertainty but gives them and their milieu compassionate and poetic treatment. A major theme is America and the best of its cultural values. The trilogy deals with this theme in a large and expansive way. It deals with the

LANFORD WILSON

passage of time, too, as do his other works, in order to express nostalgia over the loss of gentility and decency. Wilson is also a clear-eyed moralist in depicting the ways in which America has failed, and his plays can be seen as attempts to redeem that failure.

Major Works

Balm in Gilead (1965)

Wilson's first full-length play, *Balm in Gilead* has the distinction of being the first full-length original play to be staged Off Off Broadway. So successful was it when it opened on 26 January, 1965, at the Cafe La Mama Experimental Theater Club that the redoubtable Ellen Stewart was said to have stood outside every night to prevent the fire marshal from closing the overcrowded premises. Marshall W. Mason was around to direct a large cast, and the ways in which this large cast was moved around the stage and used as pieces of the mise-en-scène, as in a Chinese opera, were impressive and effective.

Wilson has likened his art to the post–Warhol new realism, and since the term *realism* will be used frequently in talking about Wilson, it is worthwhile to pause over it. In the history of the arts the term has been used to describe a method of representation, a philosophical and political attitude, and a circumscribed subject matter. Philosophically pragmatic and politically democratic, realism takes as its subject matter the here and the now, the everyday, the usual, those oppressed by circumstances. Its aesthetic aim is to represent its subject matter with meticulous fidelity to expressive detail; psychologically it would persuade the audience to think the representation is "real." The new realism in the plastic arts—notably painting—aims at rediscovering the beauty of the human form and is charged with a piercing nostalgia for the loss of a more orderly universe. Wilson has no politics to speak of, but he does have an abiding interest in the weak, the frail, the deviant, the maimed, and he is an artist who mourns losses. There is a distinct element of nostalgia running through his work. When he writes of the past, even one so morally reprehensible as, say, that of the business barons and sexual profligates of 1944 Lebanon who people *Talley & Son*, Wilson is fascinated with the period and recalls its symbols with something like affection tinged with mockery.

In a stage direction to *Balm in Gilead*, Wilson describes his cast as "the riffraff, the bums, the petty thieves, the scum, the lost, the desperate, the dispossessed, the cool."[1] The play aims to show

LANFORD WILSON

exactly what life is like in representative scenes among these Brueghelian dancers. The aesthetic reproduction of a milieu is redemptive and salvational. To achieve this aim Wilson uses as model Brecht's *Threepenny Opera*, hence the music, the lyrics, the experiments with stagecraft such as the "wall" of people used to form bits of scenery and the many intricate patterns of group activity on stage.

The central focus of the drama—the pathos of Joe and Darlene's little love affair and of Joe's tragic career as a drug pusher—seems secondary to the depiction of a whole environment. What interests Wilson are the interactions, the pointless little requests for coffee, the quick flare-ups of anger, the episodes of self-justification, need, and jealousy in the collisions of the denizens of the street corner and coffee shop that are the settings of the play.

Things—characters and subjects—change so quickly in this scenic milieu that uncertainty and transience seem to be the major themes of the play. Not only is there "no balm in Gilead,"[2] but more important there is no satisfying closure. The inhabitants of this biblical domain are in limbo.

The central metaphor for this theme is Darlene's long second-act monologue describing her life in Chicago with Cotton. To begin, although she has a regular bathroom, she "never bought one towel in all the time I lived there'' (51).[3] The climax of the tale is that she and Cotton simply didn't get married: "Something came up—one thing or another. . . . He just never got around to it"(57).

The main plot line involving Joe is also built on this uncertainty theme. Joe has made a deal with the local drug boss, Chuckles, and is about to launch into a career as a pusher in the neighborhood of the coffee shop. In act 1 he is gung-ho to undertake the enterprise, but his resolve gradually weakens and he backs out—and is killed for his indecisiveness. Similarly Joe's affair with Darlene begins on an uncertain note, a casual meeting in the coffee shop, and then drifts into closeness.

> *DARLENE*: Do you want to walk me across the street? I'd like you to.
> *JOE*: What are you, a little old lady or something?
> . . .
> *DARLENE*: I mean if you're not doing anything.

Then some talk about the weather and

> *DARLENE*: Look, I don't want you to be late for your meeting, if you're meeting someone.
> *JOE*: It isn't important. What do you have in mind?
> *DARLENE*: I don't know. Do you want to come up? You can. I'd like for you to. You know. If you want to (33–34).

Each of the three long monologues of act 1,

those of Dopey, Rake, and Fick, tend to take up this theme of uncertainty. Dopey's is in two parts (25, 26–27). The first deals with the prostitutes and their pimps. He explains that the girls take care of the pimps in order to gain a little permanence in their lives. "These guys that they ball, they aren't—around" (25), whereas the pimps are. In the second part he contrasts the longevity and adaptive capacity of roaches with those of man, and it just "burns me" (26) to think that the roaches outdo man. Rake's subject is that people are very different in different geographical locations, while Fick's is an episode describing his victimization by some thugs because he had no solid friendships to call upon to prevent such aggression.

The tonalities of the interchanges in the play all contribute to this same idea. Allegiances are constantly shifting, and the friendliness or hostility of relationships does not last. In the case of Terry, Rust, and Judy, the three lesbians, there is an almost constant jealousy motif as they accuse one another of infidelity. Even the lyrics of the central song reflect that the characters are caught in a dilemma:

> They swing, they sway,
> this cheerful crew,
> with nought to say
> and nought to do (71).

The climax of the play occurs in act 2 when the Stranger comes during the Halloween sequence and delivers crude justice to Joe by stabbing him under the heart with a needle used to inject livestock. Stage movement freezes as the scene is repeated twice. Moreover, scenes that began act 1 are also repeated here toward the end of act 2, as if to suggest the circular nature of the drama and the impossibility of a resolution.

The play is thus a dense piece of theatrical expressive realism with music, sound, light, and fancy mise-en-scène capturing the essence of this outcast society. It is easy to see the pop element in Wilson's realistic texture. At times Joe sounds much like John Garfield in a Warner Brothers 1930s "fateful" melodrama, a doomed but poetic gangster whose love for Darlene (Priscilla Lane) does not quite redeem his life. Nevertheless, like so many of this craftsman's plays, *Balm in Gilead* "works" beautifully, with distinguished and distinctive characters and a satisfying movement from beginning to end.

The Rimers of Eldritch (1967)

The Rimers of Eldritch was first presented by Theatre 1967, an offshoot of the Actors' Studio Playwrights' Unit that Edward Albee formed in association with Richard Barr and Clinton Wilder.

LANFORD WILSON

The production opened at the Cherry Lane Theatre in New York on 20 February, 1967 and was directed by Michael Kahn. It dramatizes the darker side of the Puritan ethic still flourishing in America in the 1960s in Eldritch, "a small former mining town in the Middle West; population about seventy" (6). The city of Des Moines is alluded to often enough to suggest that Eldritch is in Iowa, and Wilson's craftsmanship makes it appear as if all seventy of these Middle Americans were on stage at once. An artful set of platforms and selective lighting enmeshes the large cast in the action, which is propelled forward by a series of flashbacks from a courtroom, the scene of a one-sentence opening vignette.

An extreme example of Wilson's interest in experimenting with voices,[4] *Rimers* is in some respects a ritual cantata on the subject of scapegoating. Voices are crucial to its effects. One of the central notions carried by the singing style of these voices is that evil is literally the word of the community. What it speaks and hence believes (what it knows is immaterial) is transformed into the Word of Law and the Word of the Church (hence the same actor playing both Judge and Preacher). Ultimately these words are the propulsive force precipitating the fatal action that kills Skelly.

The play begins by dramatizing what will be one of its central ideas: that gossip, the experimental morality (or immorality) of social discourse, is a powerful mover in the affairs of a community. Lena's mother, Martha, and her friend Wilma sound the themes:

WILMA: Well, what I heard isn't fit for talk . . .

which does not stop her:

. . . but I heard that Mrs. Cora Groves, up on the highway?
MARTHA: Yes?
WILMA: Has taken a boy, she's old enough to be his mother on, and is keeping him up there in her cafe.
MARTHA: In her bed.
WILMA (With true sympathy): That woman went crazy when her husband left her.
MARTHA: Oh, I know she did.
WILMA: That woman, I swear, isn't responsible for her own actions.
MARTHA: I should say she isn't.
WILMA: I hear he does things around the cafe, whistling around like he belonged there.
MARTHA: Have you ever heard anyting like it?
WILMA: I haven't, I swear to God.

A bit of genuine sympathy is expressed, but it is soon superseded by Walter's "whistling around," a gesture of shameful liberation. Cora

LANFORD WILSON

has lied about it, too. Sexual behavior is soon seen as an aspect of evil and corruption, and the whole town is swept up in these and issues of truth and justice. As the beautifully paced drama wanders through seasons and places around the "ghost town," the focus of the myopic townspeople lands on the question of who raped the crippled Eva Jackson. It must have been Skelly, goes the common wisdom. Why Nelly Windrod is on trial is an additional piece of narrative mystery that creates suspense until very near the end. It is surprising that she shot Skelly in the accidental way she says she did it; Wilson had prepared a tangled skein of more sinister motives. Though these are not made exactly clear—Cora's repeated "She told me" (19) is never elaborated with detail—the imaginative impression remains.

Things are far more complex than Eldritch knows, believes, or even imagines. The grounded beliefs of the town are revealed to be too simple-minded. Robert Conklin's dead brother, Driver, winner of countless car races, is an imaginative center of the town's belief system. His wrecked car is a monument in the center of town, and it is an article of faith that his passing marked the beginning of the town's's decline. But he was not, after all, the stainless hero he was thought to be. He was a sadist, and an impotent one at that. Skelly is the dirty old lecher and voyeur he is alleged to be, but he does not, as is thought, poison dogs. He is, in fact, fond of them and gives them tender care. There is a hint that Josh and the Trucker do the poisoning. Moreover, Skelly's lechery is only that; the boys' ritual of taunting him with "baaas," by way of commemorating his bestiality with sheep, is inappropriate. There were plenty of human partners available to him—the lascivious Glenna Ann Reilly was only one. The evil attributed to him is only a shadow of the secret rites of corruption that he observes through the windows of Eldritch's houses and that he tells about with dramatic eloquence in his second-act monologue (37–39). Corruption is in the air of the town. Everybody breathes it. But the town does not wish to see it. As Patsy puts it; "Deformed people ought to be put out of sight. Like her [Eva] and Skelly and everybody" (30). This attitude is seen to be official doctrine when the Judge, sliding into the role of the Preacher, leads the congregation in a prayer for Skelly and Nelly Windrod: "Blind them to that dark moment and set them free, Lord" (19).

But it is precisely Wilson's point that it is part of the human condition to be "deformed," and that people cannot be "put out of sight." Thus the pattern of revelation that the play pursues. Although Patsy has seen Skelly looking in her win-

LANFORD WILSON

dow and is appropriately horrified, a further revelation by Skelly reveals that her father, Peck, "beat
the shit out of that girl of his last night. . . . Nearly
killed her" (38). The general corruption that he has
seen is ultimately more convincing than the isolated corruption the town sees residing in him
alone. For example, Patsy, who has fallen in "love"
with and plans to marry the "clean" Chuck, turns
out to be promiscuous and is heard offstage making love to Walter as the final curtain falls.

The final revelations are dramatized in act 2.
Robert Conklin is taunted by Eva into a sexual
attack which Skelly tries to stop. The action takes
place behind Windrod's Mill, and it is there that
Nelly takes out her shotgun and, confused and
aroused by the noise of the melee between Robert,
Eva, and Skelly, shoots Skelly dead. Immediately
afterward the fatal weapon is passed around
among several characters, as if to confirm what the
Judge and the Preacher have been saying all along:
it is not Nelly but the town that has been on trial.
Skelly had been ironically wrong in only one thing:
he had thought that of the two brothers, Robert
was "all right" (28). Robert lies at the trial. Eva's
mother won't believe her daughter is anyting but
pure. Cora, who has insisted all along that Skelly is
harmless, is ignored. The moral structure of the
town's beliefs remains intact.

5th of July (1978)

5th of July was given its first production by the Circle Repertory Company on 27 April, 1978[5] and ran for 168 performances. Wilson later revised it, and it was presented again on Broadway on 5 November, 1980 at the New Apollo Theatre, this time under the auspices of Jerry Arrow, Robert Lussier, and Warner Productions. Both productions were directed by Marshall W. Mason. The second run was longer than the first, and the play's reception equally enthusiastic.

The play is the first of three that Wilson has devoted to the fortunes of a family living in the vicinity of the town of Lebanon, in the farm and Bible belt of Missouri where the author was born and grew up. It depicts a special day in the lives of Ken Talley, his lover Jed, his sister June and her daughter Shirley, their old college friends John and Gwen Landis, and the Landis's friend Weston Hurley, a rock composer. In addition, a pivotal role is played by Ken and June's aunt, Sally Friedman.

The title of the play is ironic, an invitation to look at what happens the day after the birth of the American dream is celebrated. What happens is a conflict during which the lord of the family manor, Ken, who has had both legs shot off in the Vietnam war, is living there with his male lover—the rela-

LANFORD WILSON

tionship pointedly not a subject of the drama but a naturally unfolding element of the stage life like any other—withdrawn from an ordinary life of commitment as a teacher by his crippled condition. A witty, cultured man of poetic sensibility, Ken is tempted to sell the family place to a coarse, grasping, manipulative, but wealthy couple, old 1960s college friends, with the worst of whom, John Landis, he had once had sexual relations. The major theme around which the play is organized is the conflict between money, power, manipulation, deceit, and obscenity on the one hand, and culture, husbandry, sensitivity, wit, and decency on the other. To resolve this conflict Ken and Jed— and the other "good" people in the play, June, Shirley, and Sally—must overcome brutality. Ken must face his difficulties, and productivity must triumph over depraved consumption. In some of the ways that these matters are dramatized and in the way John Landis's character is set up, there is more than just the suggestion that gay relationships are on the moral side of the conflict, straight ones the other. Wilson gives John a propensity for goatish and manipulative sexual activity. Moreover, Shirley's account of John and Gwen's coupling is graphically loathsome.

There are several weaknesses in *5th of July*. The stage is rather crowded and busy with many exits and entrances, much answering of telephones and explaining of the historical connections between characters. It is not easy to believe both in the intimacy of John, Ken, and Gwen during their college days and in John's easy desertion of Ken when the three had planned to go off to Europe so that the men could escape the draft. Nor is it easy to take Ken's passivity's being so monumental that he should have then sat still and been drafted and sent to Vietnam. Further it is not easy to take his having been traumatized by the high school class refusing en masse to look at him.

Nevertheless, this is a play rich in rewards for the student of American drama and of Lanford Wilson.

Much of it is in the high-spirited style of American eccentric comedy—for example, the work of George S. Kaufman and Moss Hart—while there is another strand that derives from a major influence on Wilson: the high-strung Southern Gothic of Tennessee Williams.[6] Unlikely partners though these influences seem to be, they had in common with Wilson a nostalgia for culture and intellect and a respect for language, which they saw under attack from, say, the Philistines of *The Man Who Came to Dinner*, and the Stanley Kowalskis of this world (*A Streetcar Named Desire*). In *5th of July* culture and intellect are represented

LANFORD WILSON

by Ken and Jed; the latter is prepared to establish a baronial garden on the Talley place and take an aristocratic amount of time to do it ("it takes twenty years for a garden to mature into anything" 45). The central metaphor of the play is cultivation as it proceeds in Jed's garden, and there is a signal that something's wrong immediately when Jed enters to say that the "stupid herb garden is going rank" (7). The last word invokes Hamlet's "unweeded garden," things "rank and gross in nature / Possess it merely." Later on, there is work to be done to avoid "mildew on the phlox" (20) and control the slugs. In the meantime, what is under threat from the Landises' prospective purchase are the manorial gardens Jed has laid out, the hundred lilies waiting to bloom, and the careful gardener who has "discovered" the lost rose.

Ken is the teacher, the dry wit, the caretaker of language:

> *WESTON*: I read this book. Like about war experi-
> ences in Nam? It said shock and dope were like
> common. In the goddamned reading room; Fairleigh
> Dickinson University.
> *KEN*: [To Shirley]: I defy anyone to diagram that
> sentence.
> *WESTON*: Really heavy.
> *KEN*: The reading room . . . was heavy? Vietnam
> was heavy or the book was heavy (57–58).

The crude Landises are marked by the crudity of their language: only they use four- and five-letter obscenities, particularly Gwen:

> GWEN: (*Off*) Honey, did you call that prick in Nashville?
> JOHN: (*Off*) Negative . . .
> KEN: Did he say "negative?" Dear God (9).

Only they and their companion, Weston Hurley, call various people "doll" and pepper their speech with "like" and other locutions left over from the hip reaches of the 60s.

By contrast, the eccentrics, Sally Friedman, Ken and June's aunt, and June's daughter, Shirley, use language with, in Shirley's case, a wicked (therefore respectful) ear for parody:

> SHIRLEY: I am the last of the Talleys. And the whole family has just come to nothing at all . . . (74).

And in Aunt Sally's, a gift for accurate metaphor:

> SALLY:—I was sitting there listening to that stupid, vindictive Reverend Poole, and I looked over at that smug wife of his, always looking so pleased to have an occasion to show how easily she can cry. She was like that in school. You'd say, Francine, cry! And she'd burst into tears for you. And I looked at her and there were two of her. Sitting side by side. I just thought, Oh, my God, no. If there's one thing

LANFORD WILSON

that Lebanon does not need it's another Francine
Poole. And I was rubbing my eyes, trying to make
one of her go away. Or both of her if possible. And
I noticed that there were two Reverend Pooles giving that vacuous eulogy, and two pulpits and two
caskets and it was just all too—much. And I got up
to get the—hell out of there before there was two of
me, and—(64).

Together with Weston Hurley they make a gallery
of eccentrics that gives the play a Chekhovian
echo: a genteel old order (the Talleys), bound to
the land and its beauties as well as to culture, is
under threat of displacement by a coarse and
wealthy new order (the Landises) who threaten to
take over the beautiful land for not-so-lovely
purposes.

What has happened to the American dream is
that the generation that fought in and over Vietnam has come to this: Ken has had his legs shot off
and lives now with his vitality drawn in on itself.
June, who was once a great 60s activist, is now
doing nothing and is barely in touch with the
daughter she had by John, though she is clearly on
the side of culture in the play; where Gwen passes
around fast-food burgers and fries in act 1, June
cooks eggs and bath buns in act 2. June has had to
give Shirley to Matt and Sally to raise, and temporary custody of the girl is now being sought by the

father who won't acknowledge her. Gwen is a burned-out shell: "they took everything out by the time I was twenty-five"(29). Sally is headed for a retirement home in California with a brother and sister-in-law she can't stand. Shirley's self-drama-tization is comic and filled with charming verve, but it also suggests that her identity is at risk; with the upbringing she's had, she hardly knows who she is. What is certain is that she is far too mature for her years: she can name the sexual acts she sees and castigate her mother about June's views on "chastity."

In the end Shirley's "I am the last of the Talleys" is more than dramatization of her assum-ing the burden of the whole tribe. And Sally's buying the place speaks of a linking of generations to establish for a war survivor a modest possibility of living productively. Admittedly there is not much action in the play. But action does not put it in motion. The first act is organized around everyone's preparations to attend a little ceremony in which Sally will, a year after his cremation, dispose of her husband Matt's ashes—a ceremony that never comes off. The second act has even less action to organize it, only the question of when the Landises will be leaving. Nevertheless, Wilson's dramatic technique, the realism of Ibsen, keeps things in motion. A mysterious hint is dropped and is later enlarged upon. The incident in the classroom, for example, is mentioned several times before being explained; the issue provides suspense and promotes our interest. "Sally and I," says Jed at the beginning of act 2, "had breakfast at seven and did a few things," one of which is later revealed as spreading Matt's ashes in the garden (47). There are a number of such hints, all of which are expanded upon later. Taken together, they are the principle of dramatic action in *5th of July*.

The end of the play opens optimistic, democratic vistas: a gay couple, a precocious adolescent, a grim thirty-five-year-old mother, and a barren sixty-seven-year-old widowed aunt may survive in the renewed farmland of Missouri.

Talley's Folly (1979)

The Pulitzer Prize play for 1980 opened under what had become the usual auspices for a Lanford Wilson work, that of Marshall W. Mason, director of the Circle Repertory Company, on 3 May, 1979. Its critical reception was enthusiastic and it ran for eleven months.

Talley's Folly is the second play of Wilson's trilogy. It goes back in time to dramatize the coming together in love and marriage of Ken Talley's aunt, Sally Talley, and her husband, Matt Friedman. The drama is based on the overcoming of social distinctions and is filled with some of the same American optimism that is apparent in *5th of July*. It borders on but does not cross over into the sentimental. The play is what Matt, in his opening address to the audience, calls "a no-holds barred romantic story" (4). As such, it is in strong contrast to *5th of July*, whose Chekhovian sense of decay belies any possibility of romance.

Yet romantic as it is, the play is a piece of conventional realism in a well-crafted, easily recognized Wilsonian style—with the exception of Matt's ringmaster act. It works much like an Ibsen play, where progressive revelation of the characters' lives leads to a resolution of a dramatic problem. Here the problem is that Matt wants to undertake a relationship with Sally, who at first wants nothing to do with him.

As the play opens, Matt is in the boathouse (the Talley's folly of the title), in the sunset, "surrounded by waist-high weeds and the slender, perfectly vertical limbs of a weeping willow" (3). After his opening address to the audience, Sally enters looking for him, and the play proper begins.

Much of the play is given over to the flirtatious, teasing banter that passes appropriately between romantic lovers:

SALLY: There is no mystery.

LANFORD WILSON

MATT: Mystery isn't bad, Sally. Mystery is the spice of life.
SALLY: Variety is the spice of life.
MATT: Well, variety has always been a mystery to me (16).

Not that these two are at swords' point like Beatrice and Benedick or Katharina and Petruchio. But they are guarded and wary enough of each other to try to make verbal scores at each other's expense. This material flows in and around the solid core of the play's revelations about Matt and Sally.

The form of the play is Matt pressing against Sally's reluctance, which, because it is never quite reluctant enough to discourage Matt, only fuels his persistence.

MATT: Didn't you come to look forward to the mail [from Matt] in the morning?
SALLY: I dreaded each new day.
MATT: Now see, if I believed that, I'd leave (17).

Matt, in fact, has been given the sanguine "humor" of an Elizabethan comic character, and this is contrasted with the choleric character of Sally. Matt tries on a pair of skates and wants to waltz around in them; Sally angrily says he's stupid when he is unable to follow her skating instructions ("Sally, I'm awkward, I'm not stupid"

21). Matt waxes romantic over the beauty of the local countryside, to which Sally responds: "The weather is too dry in the summer, the crops just curl up in the field. The spring is nothing but a cycle of floods. The winters are too cold, and damp, and . . . " (18).

With superb tact Matt introduces what he knows to be the largest issue between them: that they have forbidden themselves the final intimacy of looking into each other's vulnerable hearts. This he does with the parable of the eggs. People are eggs. On one view they need to avoid bumping into each other for fear of cracking their shells. Matt's view, however, is different:

What good is an egg? Gotta be hatched or boiled or beat up into something like a lot of other eggs. Then you're cookin'. I told him he ought not to be too afraid of gettin' his yolk broke (35).

With this cue Sally begins to inquire into Matt's vulnerable secret, that of his European Jewish history, the agonies that link him to the agonies of the twentieth century. Soon afterward, at the climax of the play, Sally's themes emerge: intimacy, humanity, vulnerability. Wilson has already sounded, through her, the minor themes of money, prosperity, and how these things work out in America. Her rebelliousness, an American eccentricity that was seen fully in *5th of July*, is explained here: she has been fired from her Sunday school teaching for union-busting activities. This makes her the ideal mate for Matt, who is challenging the tax laws, making a horse the beneficiary of a trust. Pragmatic and optimistic America are seen in all this.

Matt's ringmaster act may also be called Wilson's Thornton Wilder act, which has been done in other Wilson works. For Matt resembles the stage manager/character so familiar from Wilder's plays, most notably *Our Town*. Matt's opening address to the audience along with his remark at the final curtain has several functions. It is, first, immensely theatrical. Matt's little timing gimmick, his comments to the late arrivals in the audience, and his willingness to repeat things for their benefit are sure crowd pleasers that enlist the audience's good disposition toward the play. The comic material that sets up Matt as a witty jokester has the further effect of defining the tone Wilson wants. And Matt's avowed romanticism is a way of having one's cake and eating it too; it undercuts the romance in the play, given the character he is, and reinforces it at the same time. Moreover, it demonstrates that Matt is the forceful and commanding one of the pair; his aggressive pursuit of Sally is what makes their romance possible. He literally "stages" it—and, like a master magician, does it within a prescribed time limit. In addition, this romanticism gives Wilson the opportunity to add some heavier freight to the proceedings: it is July 4, with the obvious implications of that date, and Matt is given a speech about peace, prosperity, and war—material that links Matt's and Sally's struggles to the American commonweal. *Talley's Folly* is a deceptive play in some ways, for as it rides jauntily along on the wings of romance it carries a more complex idea that does not become apparent until a later play in the trilogy.

Talley & Son (1985)

Presented first in 1981 as *A Tale Told*, the play, revised as *Talley & Son*, was re-presented under the same auspices, that of the Circle Repertory Company, with Marshall W. Mason directing, first at the Saratoga Performing Arts Festival on 8 July, 1985 and subsequently in New York on 22 November, 1985. It deals, with what is happening in the main house on the Talley place while in *Talley's Folly*, Sally Talley and Matt Friedman are working out the drama of their impending relationship down in the boathouse on that same July 4th in the year 1944. As the plays have been presented, Wilson's design and major interests have become clearer. With this work—in some ways least able to

LANFORD WILSON

stand on its own, but absorbing for the student of Wilson's work—an insight into the trilogy blooms.[7]

The plot is complicated. Eldon Talley, father of Ken, Sr., Sally, and Timmy Talley, is considering a business deal involving a clothing factory he owns jointly with Harley Campbell, Sally's former fiancé. He has arranged leaves for his sons, who are serving in front-line combat units—no easy task and a measure of his power—in order that they might share in the decision. Meanwhile Eldon's father, Calvin Stuart Talley, is thought to be near death, and the military leaves are based partly on the proximity of that event. When the curtain rises, Buddy (Kenneth Talley) and Timmy are both home, but Timmy is dead and appears on stage as a shade. The family, unaware that Timmy has been killed in the Marine assault on Tinian in the Pacific, expects him in two days.

The large cast of characters includes others only alluded to in the first two plays: Aunt Charlotte (Lottie), who encouraged Matt Friedman's suit for Sally's hand, dying of the cancer she contracted in her job painting radium dials on watches; and Buddy and his wife, Olive. There is also Sally, who rushes in and out of the house—in the first act angrily, to confront Matt in the boathouse, and at the end of the second act breathlessly, happy to run off with him.

The complication of the dramatic moment here is the introduction to Eldon's sexual depredations. A compulsive womanizer since his youth, he is confronted by Avalaine Platt, the town's seventeen-year-old sex bomb. She is his daughter by the family laundress, poor white trash Viola Platt, and she wants her due. Quietly, a silken strand of corruption appears: Buddy has been having sex with his own half sister. There have been other paternity charges against Eldon, but the patriarchal Calvin has always bailed him out. Calvin does so, breathing a high moral tone, but the play shows that he has little justification for it.

[CALVIN] TALLEY: Old Carl Saper had thirty acres of wild land. Had eighty-five black walnut trees on it. Wasn't worth nothin'. . . . Loaned him a bundle, mortgaged the land. Nine thousand dollars, fifteen years. Darn fool tried to raise geese. Didn't know the first thing about it. Feathers everywhere. Said he couldn't pay that year. Couldn't pay the interest, couldn't pay the principal; said don't take the land away, leave the land in my name and take the walnuts for payment. Black walnuts sellin' for forty cents a gunnysack, hulled. Well, sir, I went down there, looked the place over, said, "Next year you pay, this year what I can make off that thirty acres of bottom land is mine." Wrote it out, notarized by Norma Ann Comstock. Had the colored boys from Old Town pick up the walnuts, haul 'em to the ex-

LANFORD WILSON

change. Called a company in Minneapolis, Minnesota, they came here, cut down the walnut trees for fancy lumber to make veneer out of 'em. I made eleven thousand dollars out of that no count wild land in 19 and 13. Told old Saper, now you got good pasture land. I should charge you for clearing it. Fool tried to sue me. Hadn't read the paper. Read what you sign, I told him. Use your eyes. Know the worth of a thing.[8]

The seductive language of the master dramatist entertains with its accurate portrayal of character. The morals are those of a robber baron of nineteenth-century America, Lebanon, Missouri, style. But Talley is not finished. His crowning piece of chicanery is to promise Emmet a job at the clothing factory in exchange for marrying Avalaine and silencing her claims against Eldon—and then attempt to to sell off the factory so that he need not make good on the promise. This maneuver motivates an embittered Eldon to trade the factory, to which the old man is indifferent, for the bank they own, to which he is not. Nobody is sorry. For as Talley declares, "Sorry is for people who know they're doing the wrong thing while they're doing it."

Thus the trilogy finally makes its epic declaration on the shape of American morals. There is to be found in every Talley generation an abundance of iniquity (the biblical word is appropriate; Wilson quotes it in his epigraph, Psalm 90). But set off against the corruption there is an American idealist to bear witness against it, however ineffectual. The dead idealists are Calvin Talley's brother Whistler, responsible for building the boathouse (Talley's folly) and adding something to civic culture, and his dead son Stuart, the son referred to in the title of this play; the living idealist is Lottie. Sally, when she grows up to be an aunt in *5th of July*, assumes the role, energizing Ken, Jr., with her moral decency. Wilson's picture is complicated by the introduction in all the plays of strong and important characters alien to the traditional American clan. In *Talley's Folly* a European Jew, Matt, marries a native American and reorganizes the terms of the family's moral life. Similarly, in *5th of July* a homosexual, Jed, enters the Talley domain and does the same. An outsider himself, Wilson is the idealist bearing witness in the theater.

The moral fiber of the traditional South, which is to say Middle America, is clearly a large interest of the trilogy. But the play encompasses Wilson's other important interests. Like a sharp-eyed novelist, or the devotee of the new realism he acknowledges himself to be, Wilson is interested in manners, and *Talley & Son* is filled with details that dramatize these: the attitudes in 1944 toward

LANFORD WILSON

Franklin Roosevelt ("that cripple in the White House"), details of how the war is going (Buddy is the driver for Gen. Mark Clark, who commanded Allied Forces in Italy), the status of cigarette smoking, servants, the parlor of great houses, and much more. Wilson also dramatizes, through the maze of family narrative on stage, the birth of business practices now taken for granted: the battles for control of companies, mergers, the business of making money replacing the industry of making goods.

Talley & Son is the play in the trilogy that addresses public issues, broadening the privacy of and supplying a context for both *Talley's Folly* and *5th of July*. Together the plays provide fertile ground for Wilson's imaginative vision of America.

Other Works

Wilson's body of work can be thought of as an effort to construct a contemporary American myth. The elements of the myth are family narratives (as in the trilogy, *Lemon Sky*, and *The Family Continues*); dramas of community life (*The Rimers of Eldritch*, *Hot l Baltimore* and its grand hotel suite of characters, *Balm in Gilead*, *The Sand Castle* and the sensibility of California); plays on contemporary social and philosophical issues (*Serenading Louie*, describing the tragic ambience of urban yuppies, *The Gingham Dog* and its exploration of a mixed racial marriage, *Angels Fall*, about the bomb and its effects on a group of people in New Mexico); and works that delineate character with precise and penetrating insight (*The Madness of Lady Bright*, *Ludlow Fair*, *Home Free!* and *Brontosaurus*, to give only a few examples).

Beginning with the one-act form suitable to the Caffe Cino and the other performance spaces where he began, Wilson has also shown mastery of the full-length play—and beyond. Except the Talleys, his characters are mainly the socially outcast and the downtrodden, the misfits and the dispossessed of America. His preferred mode is comedy, with overtones of rueful sadness and nostalgia over the loss of a past he views with mixed emotions. His stagecraft is formidable, ranging over the use of narrators; shadow figures; experiments with sound, voices, and repeated dialogue.

The playwright has been criticized for an excess of the poetic in his language and a lack of dramatic resolution;[9] but this is to damn him for the consistent expression of his natural element—a delicate poetic language at the heart of his style—and for the absence of a dramatic neatness he has never striven for.

LANFORD WILSON

Wilson has a solid place in the study of American drama, not only because his plays "work," but because like all valuable drama they move us with their imaginative power.

Notes

1. Lanford Wilson, *Balm in Gilead and Other Plays* (New York: Hill and Wang, 1965) 3.

2. Ruby Cohn, *New American Dramatists, 1960–1980* (New York: Grove, 1983) 23.

3. Page numbers in parentheses refer to the following editions: *Balm in Gilead and Other Plays*; (Hill and Wang, 1965) *The Rimers of Eldritch and Other Plays* (New York: Dramatists Play Service, 1967); *5th of July* (Dramatists Play Service, 1982); and *Talley's Folly* (Hill and Wang, 1980).

4. Wilson is fond of using voices. See for example his *The Family Continues* and *Sextet (Yes): A Play for Voices*.

5. I give the date of the first New York production to make clear that the play was written before *Talley's Folly*.

6. Wilson was a good friend of Williams. He collaborated with him on *The Migrants*, a television play about farm workers, did a screen version of Williams's short story "One Arm," and wrote the libretto for Leo Hoiby's operatic version of *Summer and Smoke*. There is a playful but competitive allusion to Williams in this play, for Wilson's late works are heavily in Williams's debt for psychological characterization and a host of other things as well. For the allusion, see pp. 41–42 of the text.

7. The cycle of Talley plays has been projected by Wilson at possibly five plays.

8. From Wilson's MS, thus I give no page numbers. Publication is scheduled for 1987.

9. Bonnie Marranca and Gautam Dasgupta, *American Playwrights: A Critical Survey* (New York: Drama Book Specialists, 1981) 28–29; 38–39.

CHAPTER SEVEN

Playwrights at Work:
Other Voices

The five figures who have been given extended treatment in this volume are not the whole story of American drama from 1964 to 1984. In fact, when more time has elapsed, and judgment can gain the objectivity of distance, it may be that criticism will look back on this period as one of the richest in American theatrical history. Ruby Cohn, for example, surveying the period 1960–1980, discusses thirty playwrights. Bonnie Marranca and Gautam Dasgupta take on eighteen who were produced in major Off Broadway theaters before 1967, and they promise to treat more in the second volume of their critical survey. Thus this book cannot conclude without brief comment on six other playwrights.

Jack Gelber

Jack Gelber (b. 1932) has a secure place in the history of the period. *The Connection* (1959), produced by the Living Theater five years earlier than the beginning date of this study, has had far-reaching consequences for the Off Broadway and Off Off Broadway theater movements. The play concentrates on a group of junkies waiting around for Cowboy to come to their seedy apartment with a fix of heroin. Included in the group are several jazz musicians who from time to time improvise music. This is a play within a play, for there are also a couple of photographers, a producer, and a playwright named Jaybird who have come to film the proceedings and occasionally interrupt the action to comment on it: "We have selected a few addicts to improvise on Jaybird's themes."

The play is wholly in the style of this improvisation. The Pirandellian motif of a play within a play challenges the audience's orientation toward truth, theater, and reality, even going so far as to distribute the actors in the lobby during intermission—much as they are in Pirandello's *Each in His Own Way*. The action consists of the rambling stories of the actors, variations on themes of being down and out. Melodrama and comedy are present when Leach nearly dies of an overdose and Sister Salvation, whom Cowboy has picked up as a cover, is treated to a cornball comic religious rap by the addicts.

As Bonnie Marranca has remarked, the play seems tame now because its picture of junkie life has become a commonplace in the national experience.[1] But though Gelber's play relied on what he had learned from Beckett's *Waiting for Godot* and from Pirandello's technique in general, it was nevertheless an original theatrical formulation that opened new horizons for others. It was, first, an all-out attack on bourgeois values. The junkies allude to the denizens of the straight world as having addictive problems of their own. The language, the music, and the energy of the play are distinctively American, as is Gelber's important use of the film makers, a prescient vision of the insane penchant for documentation in the videotaped 80s. *The Connection* suggested to American writers who came after Gelber that plays could be set in the lowest imaginable depth and that neatly crafted works with carefully designed plots were not necessarily the standard forms of American drama. Moreover, Gelber's neutrality of tone was widely copied as a model of dramatic compassion.

Although Gelber's output has not been large and no single play of his quite the equal in vigor and freshness of *The Connection*, he has been a steady producer of works for the stage, a director in the theater, and a teacher of writing as well. His plays—*The Apple* (1961), *Square in the Eye* (1965),

OTHER VOICES

The Cuban Thing (1968), *Sleep* (1972), *Jack Gelber's New Play: Rehearsal* (1976), and *Starters* (1979)—demonstrate a continued commitment to examining social issues and joining aesthetic ones.

Amiri Baraka

Beginning at roughtly the same time as Shepard, and with equal initial force, Amiri Baraka (born LeRoi Jones in 1934), poet, novelist, playwright, Marxist, community activist, exploded onto the theatrical scene with his brilliant *Dutchman* of 1964. Nearly all of Baraka's work aims at political consequences—race war in America, the overthrow of capitalism—and thus frequently cannot avoid the tinny sound of propaganda. But the best of his works—*Dutchman* and *Slave Ship*, for example—are high imaginative art.

An ambitious play such as the *The Motion of History* (1976) is designed like a constructivist piece of Erwin Piscator's New School epic theater to move our consciousness toward a vision of Marxist America. Scenes from American history—Nat Turner's rebellion, the underground railway, Harper's Ferry—alternate with dumb show, civil rights marches, blacks at home, on the job, and in churches. Mixed media and sound montage are featured, and real people such as Ron Karenga, Roy Wilkins, and Martin Luther King, Jr. appear. But the net effect is a lesson in history and politics disguised in theater costumes. Earlier plays, produced during Baraka's black nationalist period, are equally determined to assert a message rather than dramatize a theme.

Dutchman, however, is a near perfect marriage of idea and stage action, conflict and character embodiment. The title suggests the myth of the Flying Dutchman, sailing endlessly on with his crew of the living dead, but the play creates its own myths: the "lying underbelly of the city" which is the subway; the disaster of American racism, enacted in the contest between Lula, a white woman at once a biblical temptress eating an apple and the essence of class superiority, and Clay, a black man and an intellectual with a powerful command of language.

From the start Lula (also Lulu the sexual temptress) is in command, and she exerts the force of sex, race, and violence on Clay. A black poet (he thinks he's Baudelaire) and a militant, Clay is also an assimilationist who wears a three-button suit, lives in New Jersey, and has a Wasp name. "You're a well known type," Lula tells him, with contempt. Lula mocks this aspect of his character, makes fun of his manners and ambition, and eventually uses racial slurs to goad him into beating up a white drunkard. Clay is in an agony of conflict on the issues of revolt and violence. He would, in a sense, rather be "safe with my words, and no deaths, and clean, hard thoughts urging me to new conquests."

But Lula's intent is wrapped up with his righteous anger and its consequences: they invoke and create each other's need to punish. Ultimately new subway passengers enter the car and watch Lula's dance of death, a sinuous performance punctuated with racial slurs that provoke a long, angry, and powerful rejoinder from Clay. This frightening speech provokes Lula to stab Clay, and the witnesses, the accomplice passengers, throw his body under the tracks.

Dutchman was a powerful expression of what was on America's mind and spoke to theater audiences as they had not been addressed before. It inaugurated a period when American theater would strive to speak out on a variety of subjects with the power and artistic beauty of Baraka's play. Moreover, Baraka's example has been crucial to the flowering of the black theater in America. It is hard to imagine, for example, a New Federal Theater or an Ed Bullins had Baraka not moved forward with artistry, and militancy.

UNDERSTANDING CONTEMPORARY DRAMA

Arthur Kopit

Arthur Kopit (b. 1937) is another playwright with a vision of America corrupt to the roots, its heroes finally antiheroes, its deepest life a moment of theatrical blare whose authenticity and energy is attractive but badly in need of an answerable morality to redeem it. With these central motifs Kopit's work has moved restlessly across a spectrum of private and public symbols, archetypes, and mythologies. The play that brought him to public attention, *Oh Dad Poor Dad Mama's Hung You in the Closet and I'm Feeling So Sad*, subtitled *"A Pseudoclassical Tragifarce in a Bastard French Tradition"* (1962), came to be regarded as a prime document of the theater of the absurd. *Oh Dad* created a large stir at the time, and Kopit was linked with Albee, Gelber, and Jack Richardson as one of our most promising playwrights. Since then Kopit has written more than twenty plays, including the book for the musical *Nine* and his most recent, *End of the World* (1984). But his reputation rests on *Oh Dad*; the one-acts, *The Day the Whores Came Out to Play Tennis* (1964) and *Chamber Music* (1963, rewritten for production in 1971); and what may be regarded as his major works, *Indians* (1968) and *Wings* (1978).

OTHER VOICES

The framework of *Oh Dad* is the very American problem of mother-son relations. Jonathan and his mother, Madame Rosepettle, travel the world with the corpse of the father, two Venus's flytraps, and a silver piranha fish. Madame Rosepettle is a mother with a furious need to protect her darling. Jonathan, struggling to assert his selfhood, does away with the flora and fauna but loses his equanimity and smothers Rosalie, a teen-age baby-sitter who wants him for herself, covering her body with a boy's objects: a stamp and coin collection, books. "What is the meaning of this?" Madame Rosepettle demands at the end. Bizarre and nightmarish, the question is addressed to the audience as well.

The action is grotesque comedy and the structure is parodic. Senseless and absurd, in the bourgeois-attacking tradition of Ionesco, *Oh Dad* takes the tyranny of parental protection from the Freudian cast of American interest at the time as well as from Williams's *Suddenly Last Summer*, which also features a Venus's flytrap. The impossibility of communication is also a central theme, prefiguring Kopit's lifelong interest in language as the central issue that theater must struggle with.

A slow and careful worker, Kopit produced his next substantial work, *Indians*, in 1968. In between, he had written or rewritten a number of one-acts. Inspired by an occasion in Vietnam when civilians were senselessly slaughtered, Kopit saw that the powerful could justify the horrors of their history by the creation of theatrical but nonetheless powerful mythologies. *Indians* is an imaginative dramatization of that idea.

The play is an epic of the American West, featuring Buffalo Bill Cody, his Wild West Show, and its Indians, the counterpart of television's relation to the Vietnam "Indians." Like a movie, the scenes of the drama alternate between the show itself, Indians and their altercations as they live subdued on their reservations, and presidential committees sent out to the reservation to keep the natives quiet. A narrator (mostly the journalist and author Ned Buntline, a historical figure) places in perspective Buffalo Bill's personal identity and his historical role. Quick cuts to the White House are a powerful destabilizing element. Cody is in conflict with Wild Bill Hickok over commerce and ideals. Although Buffalo Bill feels compassion for the Indians, he cannot lose his identity as an American and the drive that sends Americans to farthest shores. Nevertheless, it is an important notion of Kopit's that Cody and all the show people are forfeiting an essential part of their identities. This goes for Sitting Bull, too, whose remembered speech to his son as they walk toward the reservation is so poignant: " 'Now,' I said, 'You will never know what it is to be an Indian.' " The play is thus a play about a nation, but the playwright speaks with honorable compassion for individuals.

The theatricality of *Indians* is as impressive as the integration of the Brechtian and Pirandellian models it emulates. The glass cases with their effigies; the Western saloon with Billy the Kid and Jesse James; the Indians inpersonating wounded and dying buffaloes; the artificial horses; the monologues by the dead Indians springing suddenly to theatrical life—all contribute to make the play a permanent addition to the repertory of inspired political and mythologically made theater.

Wings was inspired by Kopit's father's suffering a stroke. Too close to his father to use him as the central character, the playwright presents the extraordinary dilemma of thought bereft of language through the consciousness of a woman past seventy, Emily Stilson, a former stunt flyer, in sections titled "Catastrophe," "Awakening," and "Explorations." The play dramatizes Emily's struggles to integrate an "intact inner self" with a diminished capacity to communicate with the outer world. As in *Chamber Music*, where Kopit expressed his obsessions with women and with flying (Amelia Earhart is a character in that play),

Wings expresses Emily's agony through images of flying. When stricken, she imagines that her plane has crashed and wonders what has happened to it. She also thinks her chute failed to open all the way and these thoughts are in a way comforting to hold on to. Though she cannot yet pronounce "plane" properly, the inner experience of knowing that she was "in my prane and crashed" is the beginning of recovery because getting it right with herself is a prelude to getting it right with the world. For such successes, language is essential.

Emily moves from being comatose and without control over impinging stimuli of sight, sound and her own voice to an elegantly controlled, linguistic tour-de-force of memory. Recalling being aloft and lost on a dark night over the American plains (a metaphor for her stroke, perhaps), she recovers her courage and direction on the wings of language. This is an enormous height above the sputtered Joycean pun: of a toothbrush, she had said: "toovebram, toove-britch bratch brush bridge, two-bridge." This struggle to overcome a fatal, living silence gives *Wings* enormous power. The beauty of the play, however, rests also on the linguistic pyrotechnics through which Kopit portrays Emily's passages. It is language, after all, that Arthur Kopit sees as the essential human characteristic, and his theater expresses that belief with consistent poetic verve.

Adrienne Kennedy

Language is not the be-all for others, however. *Funnyhouse of a Negro* (1964), by Adrienne Kennedy (b. 1931), was only the third play by a black woman to open in New York. Like all of Kennedy's work it is a delicate blend of surrealism and expressionism, a drama of inner states made manifest on stage through astonishing images of dream and vision.

The setting of the first scene is bizarre, Daliesque. Before the play begins, "a woman dressed in a white nightgown walks across the stage carrying before her a bald head." Just as she vanishes, the curtain opens, "a cheap material and a ghastly white, a material that brings to mind the interior of a cheap casket; parts of it are frayed and it looks as if it has been gnawed by rats." Death stalks the play in the manner of a dream. The stage directions for the first scene call for great black ravens flying, royal gowns of white, headpieces of frizzy hair, motionless performers, dead-white faces. The two women, Queen Victoria and the Duchess of Hapsburg, share an identity. Both were "made" by the rape perpetrated by their black father on a white woman, Queen Victoria (though one of them is, simultaneously, Queen Victoria). Now the Negro, a black female with a hangman's noose around her neck, appears and begins to recite a long monologue identifying her home as the top floor of a brownstone in the West Nineties in New York and herself a contemporary black girl, an English major in college, like her mother in Atlanta. Shades of skin color are on her mind. She complains of her frizzy head of hair, the hair we see protruding from masks. She is in love with Raymond, who is Jewish and loves Negroes.

Jesus, "a hunchback, yellow-skinned dwarf," and Patrice Lumumba, whose "head appears to be split in two with blood and tissue in eyes" and carrying "an ebony mask," also appear. The Negro identifies herself with these, as well as with Queen Victoria and the Duchess. The Negro is also Sarah, whose home is the funnyhouse, dominated by a white landlady and her white lover. These fragmented selves carry on dialogue and monologue in the funnyhouse. The themes are the jungle of black identity, rape, murder, suicide; whites against and constrained by blacks; whites for and with blacks. The play ends very nearly as it began, with a black woman hanging in the funnyhouse and a black man knocking at the door.

Kennedy's unique dramatic style is bravely

pursued in *The Owl Answers* (1965) and *The Rat's Mass* (1968). Black women are fragmented by conflicting claims of origin and identity, acting out in densely allusive speech, poetic metaphors, and animal imagery what it feels like in the interior dream countries of love and hate and good and evil. *A Beast Story* (1969) mixes a deep vein of animal imagery and personification with rape and murder. *A Lesson in Dead Language* (1968) is really a lesson in the depths of lost ritual. The play is set in an ordinary classroom with an extraordinary teacher; from the waist up she is a white dog, speaking to seven white-clad little girls a lesson on bleeding initiated by the death of a white dog. Red stains spreading on white organdy—Kennedy is able to make mesmeric images out of ordinary pieces of cloth—suggest the rite of menstruation and the passage from childhood to maturity entailed in the moving blood. The work of a uniquely gifted dramatist, Kennedy's plays are unreasonably neglected.

Jean-Claude Van Itallie

Another dramatist whose reputation does not match his accomplishments, Jean-Claude Van Itallie was born in Belgium in 1936 but grew up on

Long Island. He and Megan Terry are the playwrights best known for their association with the
Open Theater. Van Itallie, associated for most of
his career with the Open Theater, which he joined
in 1963, is a playwright of high seriousness. He
conceives of the gathering of audience and players
as a sacrament of functioning "to bring people
together in a community ceremony where the
actors are in some sense priests or celebrants, and
the audience is drawn to participate with the actors
in a kind of eucharist."[2]

His *America Hurrah* is a tryptych of three short
works—*Interview*, *TV*, and *Motel*—that sets side by
side devastating images of reductive, mechanical,
and dehumanized America. *Interview*, subtitled "*A
Fugue for Eight Actors*," is a rondo featuring four
applicants and four interviewers doing banal questions and answers that break apart into leapfrog-
ging and other acrobatics. A chorus aligns itself
against actors transformed (using Chaikin's exercise technique of transformation) into different
character types in successive scenes. The actors,
who become priest-confessant, psychiatrist-patient
("Blah, blah, blah, blah, blah, blah, *hostile*/Blah,
blah, blah, blah, blah, blah *penis*"), align themselves against the audience. They become parts of
a machine and give us an image of a mechanical
culture.

OTHER VOICES

TV, which takes place in a television control booth, juxtaposes life and video. *Motel* features three actors in doll masks, and its action is literally the destruction not only of the room but of one of the dolls as well. Naturally, the victim is the motel-keeper.

Perhaps the most important of Van Itallie's works is, ironically, one that cannot be wholly appreciated with reference to a text. *The Serpent* (1968) was the first entirely collaborative effort of the Open Theatre. Subtitled "A Ceremony," depended for its charm and power on this close collaboration. For the production exploited its universal motifs of creation, sin, pride, corruption, and violence within a muscial structure in which actors and verse text, chorus and choreographed movement, created not just the physical serpent of Genesis but the snake within recent American history.

Part of the performance is the opening exercises of the actors—suggesting the extratheatricality of the event. There follows a procession of actors through the audience, and three times the group are frozen in tableaux of key images from the play, suggesting the overture to an opera. There are reenactments of the Kennedy and King assassinations; Kennedy's wife is seen climbing over the back of the car to cradle his head, but history is a living presence because the play begins with an autopsy and a gunshot, suggesting what is to come and what has passed. As a parallel there is a segue into Martin Luther King, Jr.'s "I have a dream" speech, and there are returns to the Garden of Eden. When Adam bites the apple, apples are distributed to the audience.

Marsha Norman

Among the most promising of the younger playwrights is Marsha Norman, whose *'night, Mother* won the Pulitzer Prize for drama in 1983. Norman was born in Louisville, Kentucky, in 1947 and began her career with *Getting Out* (1978), first produced by the Actors Theater of Louisville. It is a beautifully expressive first play that explores without polemical fervor but with considerable dramatic power, ingenuity, and down-home wit something of what it means to be a woman in America in the 1980s. The work is built on alternating scenes that contrast the lives of Arlene Holsclaw, just getting out of prison, rehabilitated, after serving eight years for murder, and Arlene's younger, unregenerate self—Arlie—who is on stage as a figment of Arlene's memory. Arlie is a memory that, the playwright says, "will not go

OTHER VOICES

away." The play is meant to dramatize the transformation of Arlie's explosive, defiant anger into something more like Arlene's ordinary but socially acceptable ambition: a decent job and a reconciliation with her illegitimate son, Joey. To realize this ambition—which, in the context of her previous life, is like reaching for the moon—Arlene must give up hostility toward others, reconcile herself with women, especially a mother figure, and see men for what they have been in her life.

The contrast between Arlie and Arlene produces eloquent and moving theater, but the full depth and complexity of *Getting Out* come also from the playwright's exploration of Arlie/Arlene's relationships to institutions and their impersonal controlling power.[3] In these relationships there is no contrast between the two women; both are victims.

Arlene is nearly raped by Bennie, a guard who accompanies her to Louisville from prison in Alabama, because he cannot forgo the voyeuristic access to her body that was his institutional privilege in the prison. It is only when Arlene has reconciled herself to her neighbor Ruby, also an ex-convict, and shucked off the exploitative grasp of her former pimp and lover, Carl, that she can give vent to what Norman shows is her free artistic bent as a human being. Surrealist and real, the play is powerful theater.

The title *'night, Mother* refers to the heroine's, Jessie's, suicidal farewell. The whole of the play enacts the preparations that Jessie suddenly and shockingly declares herself to be making as the curtain rises. Without employing the surrealist double action of *Getting Out*, *'night, Mother* dramatizes ancillary themes. Arlie's anger is tamed, and she lives; Jessie's buried anger is not, and she kills herself in an act of simultaneous self-loathing and liberation, perhaps the sole act of independence she is capable of.

Along the way Norman dramatizes and gives voice to the unheard, the blue-collar world that is the counterpart in drama of those who people the fictional worlds of Bobbie Ann Mason, Jayne Anne Phillips, and Raymond Carver. Jessie has epileptic fits, and these are powerful symbols of powerlessness, the darkness that envelops the quiet women, those who live in rural bungalows and give each other manicures on Saturday nights. Just as Jessie blacks out on her mother from time to time, to that woman's humorous chagrin, so she has, like all women, moments of crucial unconsciousness. In this beautifully blameless drama the men in the family hold the power even when they are not on stage and even when they are most admired. It is the woman's tragic fate to almost enjoy—an energetic suicide.

Norman's other works—three more full-length and three one-acts—have often been produced in regional theaters around the country. They show a diversity of interests, from the question of religious faith to the magic of frontier narrative.

But then there are still more voices at work in our theater. The whole enterprise of American playwriting, as has been emphasized here, has been abundant. In fact, it continues to be rich and diverse and significant enough to require the making of more books—and soon.

Notes

1. Bonnie Marranca and Gautam Dasgupta, *American Playwrights: A Critical Survey* (New York: Drama Book Specialists, 1981) 137.

2. C. W. E. Bigsby, *A Critical Introduction to Twentieth-Century American Drama* (New York: Cambridge University Press, 1985) 3:114–15.

3. Timothy Murray analyzes this theme with cogency. See his "Patriarchal Panopticism, or the Seduction of a Bad Joke: *Getting Out* in Theory," *Theatre Journal* 35 (1983): 376–88.

Bibliography

For each writer, under primary sources there are listed both plays and movie or television scripts. The plays are given in alphabetical order, the scripts by date. For each play dates of first production and first New York production are given in parentheses. A date alone within the parentheses indicates date of composition; the play has not been produced. A question marks indicates that information on date of composition or productions is unavailable. The printed source or sources follow the parentheses. For film and TV scripts, dates are either air dates or the years of theatrical release. The secondary sources are highly selective.

Except where indicated, the "General Works" section covers the whole subject area of this book rather than individual playwrights.

The standard bibliographical source in the field of contemporary American drama is the "American" section of Charles A. Carpenter, *Modern Drama Studies: An Annual Bibliography*, published every year since 1974 by the journal *Modern Drama*. From 1964 to 1973 the *PMLA* Annual Bibliography should be consulted. These journals are supplemented by Kimball King, *Ten Modern Amer-*

BIBLIOGRAPHY

ican Playwrights: An Annotated Bibliography (New York and London: Garland, 1982) and by Phyllis Johnson Kaye, *The National Playwrights' Register*, 2nd ed. (Waterford, CT: Eugene O'Neill Theater Center, 1981), which lists primary but not secondary sources. Much of the Ed Bullins material is taken from Hatch and Abdullah, eds., *Black Playwrights 1823–1977: An Annotated Bibliography* (New York: Bowker, 977).

Ed Bullins

Primary Sources: Plays

The American Flag Ritual (1969). Ed Bullins. *The Theme Is Blackness:* The Corner *and Other Plays.* New York: Morrow, 1973.

Black Commercial #2 (1972). Ed Bullins. *The Theme Is Blackness:* The Corner *and Other Plays.* New York: Morrow, 1973.

Clara's Ole Man (San Francisco, 1965; New York, 1968). *Five Plays by Ed Bullins.* Indianapolis: Bobbs-Merrill, 1969. Albert Poland and Bruce Mailman, eds. *The Off Off Broadway Book.* Indianapolis: Bobbs-Merrill, 1972.

The Corner (Boston, 1968; New York, 1970). Ed Bullins. *The Theme Is Blackness:* The Corner *and Other Plays.* New York: Morrow, 1973. Woodie King, Jr., and Ron Milner, eds. *Black Drama Anthology.* New York: Columbia Univ. Press, 1972.

Daddy (New York, 1977). Manuscript.

Deathlist (New York, 1970). Ed Bullins. *Four Dynamite Plays.* New York: Morrow, 1972.

Dialect Determinism (or The Rally) (San Francisco, 1965; New

BIBLIOGRAPHY

York, 1968). Ed Bullins. *The Theme Is Blackness:* The Corner *and Other Plays.* New York: Morrow, 1973.

Do-Wah (?). Musical. Manuscript.

The Duplex: A Black Love Fable in Four Movements (New York, 1970). New York: Morrow, 1971.

The Electronic Nigger: (New York, 1968). *Five Plays by Ed Bullins.* Indianapolis: Bobbs-Merrill, 1969.

The Fabulous Miss Marie (New York, 1971). Ed Bullins, ed. *The New Lafayette Theatre Presents: Plays with Aesthetic Comments by 6 Black Playwrights.* Garden City, NY: Anchor, 1974.

The Game of Adam and Eve (With Shirley Tarbell; Boston, 1969). Manuscript.

The Gentleman Caller (New York, 1969). Clinton F. Oliver, ed. *Contemporary Black Drama.* New York: Scribner's, 1971. *Black Quartet,* by Ben Caldwell and Others, New York: Signet, 1970.

Goin' a Buffalo (New York, 1968). *Five Plays by Ed Bullins.* Indianapolis: Bobbs-Merrill, 1969. James V. Hatch, ed. *Black Theater U.S.A.* New York: Free Press, 1974. William Couch, ed. *New Black Playwrights.* New York: Avon, 1970.

The Helper (New York, 1970). Ed Bullins. *The Theme Is Blackness:* The Corner *and Other Plays.* New York: Morrow, 1973.

Home Boy (New York, 1976). Music by Aaron Bell. Manuscript.

House Party (New York, 1973). Manuscript.

How Do You Do? (San Francisco, 1965). LeRoi Jones and Larry Neal, eds. *Black Fire.* New York: Morrow, 1968.

I Am Lucy Terry (New York, 1976). Manuscript.

In New England Winter (New York, 1971). Ed Bullins, ed. *New Plays from the Black Theater.* New York: Bantam, 1969.

In the Wine Time (New York, 1968). *Five Plays by Ed Bullins.*

BIBLIOGRAPHY

Indianapolis: Bobbs-Merrill, 1969. Lindsay Patterson, comp. *Black Theater.* New York: Dodd, Mead, 1971. John Lahr and Jonathan Price, eds. *The Great American Life Show: 9 Plays from the Avant-Garde Theater.* New York: Bantam: 1974.

It Bees Dat Way (London, 1971; New York, 1976). Ed Bullins. *Four Dynamite Plays.* New York: Morrow, 1972.

It Has No Choice (San Francisco, 1966). Ed Bullins. *The Theme Is Blackness:* The Corner *and Other Plays.* New York: Morrow, 1973.

Jo Anne! (New York, 1976). Manuscript.

Malcolm: 71; or Publishing Blackness (1971). *The Black Scholar* 6.9 (1975).

The Man Who Dug Fish (New York, 1970). Ed Bullins. *The Theme Is Blackness:* The Corner *and Other Plays.* New York: Morrow, 1973.

Michael (New York, 1978). Manuscript.

A Minor Scene (San Francisco, 1966). Ed Bullins. *The Theme Is Blackness:* The Corner *and Other Plays.* New York: Morrow, 1973.

The Mystery of Phyllis Wheatley (New York, 1976). Manuscript.

Next Time (1972). *Spirit: The Magazine of Black Culture* 1.1 (1975).

Night of the Beast (1969). Ed Bullins. *Four Dynamite Plays.* New York: Morrow, 1972.

One Minute Commercial (1969). Ed Bullins. *The Theme Is Blackness:* The Corner *and Other Plays.* New York: Morrow, 1973.

The Pig Pen (New York, 1970). Ed Bullins. *Four Dynamite Plays.* New York: Morrow, 1972.

The Play of the Play (1970). Ed Bullins. *The Theme Is Blackness:* The Corner *and Other Plays.* New York: Morrow, 1973.

BIBLIOGRAPHY

Sepia Star (New York, 1977). Music and lyrics by Mildred Kayden. Manuscript.

A Short Play for a Small Theatre (1971). Ed Bullins. *The Theme Is Blackness:* The Corner *and Other Plays.* New York: Morrow, 1973. *Black World* 2.6 (1971).

A Son, Come Home (New York, 1968). *Five Plays by Ed Bullins.* Indianapolis: Bobbs-Merrill, 1969.

State Office Building Curse (1969). Ed Bullins. *The Theme Is Blackness:* The Corner *and Other Plays.* New York: Morrow, 1973.

Storyville (La Jolla, 1977). Music and lyrics by Mildred Kayden. Manuscript.

A Street Play (1970). Ed Bullins. *The Theme Is Blackness:* The Corner *and Other Plays.* New York: Morrow, 1973.

Street Sounds (New York, 1970). Ed Bullins. *The Theme Is Blackness:* The Corner *and Other Plays.* New York: Morrow, 1973.

The Taking of Miss Janie (New York, 1975). Manuscript.

The Theme Is Blackness (San Francisco, 1966; New York, 1973). Ed Bullins. *The Theme Is Blackness:* The Corner *and Other Plays.* New York: Morrow, 1973.

We Righteous Bombers (1968? A completion of the work of Kingsley B. Bass, Jr.). Ed Bullins, ed. *New Plays from the Black Theater.* New York: Bantam, 1969.

You Gonna Let Me Take You Out Tonight, Baby? (1969). Ahmad Alhimisi and Harun Wangara, eds. *Black Arts.* Detroit: Black Arts Publishing, 1969.

Primary Sources: Screenplays

The Box Office (1970). Short script. Ed Bullins, ed. *Black Theatre* 3 (1970).

BIBLIOGRAPHY

Secondary Sources

Anderson, Jervis. "Profiles: Dramatist." *New Yorker* 16 June 1973: 40–79. A long biographical essay detailing Bullins's development as a playwright and his relations with the New Lafayette and black politics and theater in general.

Andrews, W. D. E. "Theater of Black Reality: The Blues Drama of Ed Bullins." *Southwest Review* 65 (1979): 78–90. Argues that unlike Baraka, who cannot help but engage white society in one way or another, Bullins concentrates on black society exclusively, making an "Orphic" descent into the black ghetto to grasp the essence of a culture and transform it into poetry. Analyzes *Clara's Ole Man* and *In New England Winter*.

Bernstein, Samuel J. "*The Taking of Miss Janie.*" *The Strands Entwined: A New Direction in American Drama.* Boston: Northeastern University Press, 1980. Summary of the critical reception and analysis of this provocative play.

Blackman, Brandon R. IV. "Black Hope of Broadway." *Sepia* 24 (Dec. 1975): 62–68. A survey of Bullins's career and an analysis of his status in the theater.

Bruck, Peter. "Ed Bullins: The Quest and Failure of an Ethnic Community Theatre." *Essays in Contemporary American Drama.* Ed. Hedwig Bock and Albert Wertheim. Munich: Hueber, 1981. 123–140. Discusses the politics of ghetto hustling as a key element in Bullins's drama and concludes that the work has "revitalized the black stage" despite the failure of the New Lafayette.

Cohn, Ruby. *New American Dramatists: 1960–1980.* New York: Grove, 1982. Contains a brief but accurate account of Bullins's career with incisive analyses of the major works.

Gussow, Mel. "Bullins, the Artist and the Activist, Speaks." *New York Times* 22 Sept. 1971: 44. Reports on an interview with Bullins in which he speaks of himself as a public persona.

Jeffers, Lance. "Bullins, Baraka and Elder: The Dawn of Grandeur in Black Drama." *College Language Association Journal* 16,1 (1972): 32–48. Claims that Bullins leads the way toward this grandeur through an unsparing, unsentimental, yet subtle and sympathetic analysis of black life in such plays as *Clara's Ole Man* and *In the Wine Time.*

Kerr, Walter. "Mr. Bullins Is Himself at Fault." *New York Times* 19 Mar. 1972. Sec. 2:1, 7. Takes Bullins to task for the playwright's dissatisfaction with *The Duplex*, criticizing the play and not the production.

Munk, Erika. "Up from Politics: An Interview with Ed Bullins." *Performance #2* (Apr. 1972): 52–60. Ranges across topics that include Bullins's life, politics, association with the New Lafayette, black aesthetics, and much more.

Riley, Clayton. "Bullins: 'It's Not the Play I Wrote.'" *New York Times* 19 Mar. 1972. Sec. 2:1, 7. Gives Bullins's side of *The Duplex* controversy.

Tener, Robert L. "Pandora's Box: A Study of Ed Bullins' Dramas." *College Language Association Journal* 19 (1976): 533–44. A study of the social setting, the values and mores of the characters and their lives, that accounts for the form of his plays in which the characters are boxed in.

True, Warren R. "Ed Bullins, Anton Chekhov and the 'Drama of Mood.'" *College Language Association Journal* 20 (1977): 521–32. A detailed study of the parallels between the two playwrights.

BIBLIOGRAPHY

David Mamet

Primary Sources: Plays

All Men are Whores: An Inquiry (New Haven, 1977). David Mamet. *Short Plays and Monologues*. New York: Dramatists Play Service, 1981.

American Buffalo (Chicago, 1975; New York, 1976). New York: Samuel French, 1977; New York: Grove Press, 1977. A condensed version appears in *Best Plays of 1976–1977*. Ed. Otis Guernsey. New York: Dodd, Mead, 1977.

The Blue House: City Sketches (?). David Mamet. *Short Plays and Monologues*. New York: Dramatists Play Service, 1981.

Dark Pony (New Haven, 1977; New York, 1979). *Reunion and Dark Pony: Two Plays*. New York: Grove, 1979. *Reunion, Dark Pony, The Sanctity of Marriage: Three Plays*. New York: Samuel French, 1979.

Duck Variations (Plainfield, VT, 1972; New York, 1975). New York: Samuel French, 1971. *Sexual Perversity in Chicago and Duck Variations*. New York: Grove, 1978. *Best Short Plays*. Ed. Stanley Richards. New York: Chilton, 1977.

Edmond (Chicago, 1982; New York, 1982). New York: Samuel French, 1983.

Glengarry Glen Ross (London, 1983; New York, 1984). New York: Grove, 1984.

In Old Vermont (?). David Mamet. *Short Plays and Monologues*. New York: Dramatists Play Service, 1981.

Lakeboat (Marlboro, VT, 1970). New York: Grove, 1981; New York: Samuel French, 1983.

Litko: A Dramatic Monologue (Chicago, 1973). David Mamet. *Short Plays and Monologues*. New York: Dramatists Play Service, 1981.

A Life in the Theatre (New York, 1978). New York: Grove, 1978.

BIBLIOGRAPHY

Lone Canoe (Chicago, 1979). Manuscript.

Mackinac (New York, 1977). Children's play. Manuscript.

Mr. Happiness (New York, 1978). *The Water Engine and Mr. Happiness: Two Plays.* New York: Grove, 1978, New York: Samuel French, 1978.

The Poet and the Rent (Chicago, 1972; New York, 1974). New York: Samuel French, 1981.

Prairie du Chien (radio play; NPR, 1979). David Mamet. *Short Plays and Monologues.* New York: Dramatists Play Service, 1981.

Red River (San Francisco, 1982). Manuscript.

Reunion (Chicago, 1976; New York, 1979). *Reunion and Dark Pony: Two Plays.* New York: Grove, 1979. *Reunion, Dark Pony, The Sanctity of Marriage: Three Plays.* New York: Samuel French, 1979.

The Revenge of the Space Pandas or Bunky Rudich and the Two Speed Clock (Chicago, 1977). Children's play. Chicago: The Dramatic Publishing Company, 1983.

The Sanctity of Marriage (New York, 1979). *Reunion, Dark Pony, The Sanctity of Marriage: Three Plays.* New York: Samuel French, 1979.

A Sermon (Chicago, 1979; New York, 1981). David Mamet. *Short Plays and Monologues.* New York: Dramatists Play Service, 1981.

Sexual Perversity in Chicago (Chicago, 1974; New York, 1975). New York: Samuel French, 1977. *Sexual Perversity in Chicago and Duck Variations.* New York: Grove, 1978.

Shoeshine (New York, 1978). David Mamet. *Short Plays and Monologues.* New York: Dramatists Play Service, 1981.

Squirrels (Chicago, 1971; New York, 1972). New York: Samuel French, 1982.

The Water Engine (Chicago, 1977; New York, 1977). *The Water*

BIBLIOGRAPHY

Engine and Mr. Happiness: Two Plays. New York: Grove, 1978; New York: Samuel French, 1982.

The Woods (1977). New York: Grove, 1979; New York: Samuel French, 1979.

Primary Sources: Filmscripts

The Postman Always Rings Twice (1981).
The Verdict (1983).

Secondary Sources

Barbera, Jack V. "Ethical Perversity in America: Some Observations on David Mamet's *American Buffalo.*" *Modern Drama* 24.3 (1981): 270–75. Sees the value of the play in its rich language that motivates the characters' behavior, its comment on American business, and its existential thematic content.

Christiansen, Richard. "The Young Lion of Chicago Theater." *Chicago Tribune Magazine* 11 July 1982: 11–16. The story of Mamet's entry into Chicago theater and his development as a playwright.

Ditsky, John. "'He Lets You See the Thought There': The Theater of David Mamet." *Kansas Quarterly* 12.4 (1980): 25–34. Mamet's work is the epitome of the "theater of inarticulation" as influenced by Harold Pinter. Play-by-play analyses of the works up to 1980.

Freedman, Samuel G. "The Gritty Eloquence of David Mamet." *New York Times Magazine* 21 April 1985: 32, 40, 42, 46, 50, 51, 64. A biographical essay tracing the development of Mamet's vocation and his growing reputation.

Gale, Stephen H. "David Mamet: The Plays, 1972–1980." *Essays in Contemporary American Drama*, Ed. Hedwig Bock and Albert Wertheim. Munich: Hueber, 1981: 207–33. An astute critical survey of Mamet's career.

BIBLIOGRAPHY

Mamet, David. "Why I Write for Chicago Theater." *Vanity Fair* Nov. 1984: 52–53. A personal statement about the authentic vitality of Chicago theater and its influence on Mamet.

Schleuter, June, and Elizabeth Forsyth. "America as Junkshop: The Business Ethnic in David Mamet's *American Buffalo*." *Modern Drama* 26.4 (1983): 492–500. An analysis of business as the central issue in the play.

Storey, Robert. "The Making of David Mamet." *Hollins Critic* 16.4 (1979): 1–11. A survey of the writer's work emphasizing a major theme in all his works of "invidious American greed."

Zehme, Bill, "Hot Chicago." *Vanity Fair* Nov. 1984: 50–55; 114–15. On the Chicago theater revival from 1974 to 1984, featuring much material on Mamet's connections to theater in the city.

David Rabe

Primary Sources: Plays

The Basic Training of Pavlo Hummel (New York, 1971). *The Basic Training of Pavlo Hummel and Sticks and Bones: Two Plays.* New York: Viking, 1973; New York: Penguin, 1978.

Goose and Tom Tom (New York, 1982). Manuscript.

Hurlyburly (New York, 1984). New York: Grove, 1985.

In the Boom Boom Room (New York, 1973). New York: Samuel French, 1975.

The Orphan (New York, 1973; final version Philadelphia, 1974). New York: Samuel French, 1975.

Sticks and Bones (Philadelphia, 1969; New York, 1971). New York: Samuel French, 1979. *The Basic Training of Pavlo Hummel and Sticks and Bones: Two Plays.* New York: Viking, 1973; New York: Penguin, 1978.

BIBLIOGRAPHY

Streamers (New York, 1976). New York: Samuel French, 1978. New York: Athenaeum, 1977.

Secondary Sources

Adler, Thomas B. "'The Blind Leading the Blind': Rabe's *Sticks and Bones* and Shakespeare's *King Lear*." *Papers on Language and Literature* 15.2 (1979): 203–06. An analysis of the central imagery of sight and blindness and its relation to parallels in Shakespeare's *Lear*.

Asahina, Robert. "The Basic Training of American Playwrights: Theater and the Vietnam war." *Theater* 9.2 (1977): 30–37. A survey of the significant drama dealing with the Vietnam war. Rabe's trilogy is discussed: *Pavlo* and *Sticks and Bones* are criticized and *Streamers* praised.

Bernstein, Samuel J. *"Sticks and Bones." The Strands Entwined: A New Direction in American Drama.* Boston: Northeastern University Press, 1980. An analysis of the play that describes it as depicting the "ethnocentric cruelty of American culture" through an amalgam of realistic and expressionistic theatrical technique.

"A Conversation Between Neil Simon and David Rabe: The Craft of the Playwright." *New York Times Magazine* 26 May 1985: 36–38, 52, 56–57, 60–62. Rabe talks about his work habits, how the process of writing lays hold of him, what inspires him, his aesthetic ideas.

Freedman, Samuel G. "Rabe and the War at Home." *New York Times* 28 June 1984: C13. On the relations of themes in *Hurlyburly* to previous plays.

Hertzbach, Janet S. "The Plays of David Rabe: A World of Streamers." *Essays in Contemporary American Drama.* Ed. Hedwig Bock and Albert Wertheim. Munich: Hueber, 1981. 173–86. A first-rate introduction to Rabe, emphasizing the destructive propensities of the characters in terms of the central motif of *Streamers*.

Homan, Sidney. "American Playwrights in the 1970's: Rabe and Shepard." *Critical Quarterly* 24.1 (1982): 73–82. Selects Rabe and Shepard as the dominating figures in American playwriting of the 70s through brief analyses of Rabe's Vietnam trilogy and three late plays of Shepard: *True West*, *Curse of the Starving Class*, and *Buried Child*.

Phillips, Jerrold A. "A Descent into the Abyss: The Plays of David Rabe." *West Virginia University Papers on Philology* 25 (1979): 108–17. Considers Rabe's work through *Streamers* as powerful expressions of the existential meaninglessness of life.

Rosen, Carol. *Plays of Impasse: Contemporary Drama Set in Confining Institutions*. Princeton: Princeton University Press, 1983. Includes analyses of *Pavlo Hummel* and *Streamers*; that they are set in the "total institution" of the military leads inevitably to the "claustrophobic, no-exit situation" in each.

Sam Shepard

Primary Sources: Plays

Action (New York, 1975). *Fool for Love and Other Plays*. New York: Bantam, 1984. *Angel City and Other Plays*. New York: Urizen, 1976.

Angel City (San Francisco, 1976; New York, 1984). *Angel City and Other Plays*. New York: Urizen, 1976. *Fool for Love and Other Plays*. New York: Bantam, 1984.

Back Bog Beast Bait (New York, 1971). *The Unseen Hand and Other Plays*. Indianapolis: Bobbs-Merrill, 1972.

Blue Bitch (London, 1972). Radio play. Manuscript.

BIBLIOGRAPHY

Buried Child (San Francisco, 1978, New York, 1978). *Sam Shepard: Seven Plays*. New York: Bantam, 1981.

Chicago (New York, 1965). *Chicago and Other Plays*. New York: Urizen Books, 1967. Nick Orzel and Michael Smith, eds. *Eight Plays from Off-Off Broadway*. Indianapolis: Bobbs-Merrill, 1966.

Cowboy Mouth (Edinburgh, 1971; New York, 1971). *Fool for Love and Other Plays*. New York: Bantam, 1984. *Angel City and Other Plays*. New York: Urizen, 1976.

Cowboys (New York, 1964). Never published. No copy exists.

Cowboys #2 (New York, 1967). *Angel City and Other Plays*. New York: Urizen, 1976.

Curse of the Starving Class (London, 1977; New York, 1978). *Angel City and Other Plays*. New York: Urizen, 1976. *Sam Shepard: Seven Plays*. New York: Bantam, 1981.

Dog (New York, 1965). Manuscript.

Fool for Love (San Francisco, 1983; New York, 1984). *Fool for Love and Other Plays*. New York: Bantam, 1984.

Forensic and the Navigators (New York, 1967). *The Unseen Hand and Other Plays*. Indianapolis: Bobbs-Merrill, 1972.

4-H Club (New York, 1965). *The Unseen Hand and Other Plays*. Indianapolis: Bobbs-Merrill, 1972. *Angel City and Other Plays*. New York: Urizen, 1976.

Fourteen Hundred Thousand (Minneapolis, 1966). *Chicago and Other Plays*. New York: Urizen, 1967.

Geography of a Horse Dreamer (London 1974). *Fool for Love and Other Plays*. New York: Bantam, 1984.

The Holy Ghostly (On tour, 1969). *The Unseen Hand and Other Plays*. Indianapolis: Bobbs-Merrill, 1972.

Icarus's Mother (New York, 1965). *Chicago and Other Plays*. New York: Urizen, 1967.

Inacoma. (San Francisco 1977). Manuscript.

BIBLIOGRAPHY

Jacaranda. (1979). Videotape; performed by the dancer Daniel Nagrin from a few pages of script by Shepard.

Killer's Head (New York, 1975). *Angel City and Other Plays.* New York: Urizen, 1976.

La Turista (New York, 1967). *Sam Shepard: Seven Plays.* New York: Bantam, 1981.

A Lie of the Mind (New York, 1985). Manuscript.

Little Ocean (London, 1974). Manuscript.

The Mad Dog Blues (New York, 1971). *Angel City and Other Plays.* New York: Urizen, 1976.

Melodrama Play (New York, 1967). *Chicago and Other Plays.* New York: Urizen, 1967. *Fool for Love and Other Plays.* New York: Bantam, 1984.

Nightwalk New York, 1973. contributor, with Megan Terry and Jean-Claude Van Itallie. Manuscript.

Operation Sidewinder (New York, 1970). *The Great American Life Show: 9 Plays from the Avant-Garde Theater,* Ed. John Lahr and Jonathan Price. New York: Bantam, 1974.

Red Cross (New York, 1966). *Chicago and Other Plays.* New York: Urizen, 1967.

The Rock Garden (New York, 1964). *Angel City and Other Plays.* New York: Urizen, 1976.

Rocking Chair (New York, 1965). Manuscript.

The Sad Lament of Pecos Bill on the Eve of Killing His Wife (San Francisco, 1970). *Theatre* 12.3 (1981): 32–38.

Savage/Love (San Francisco, 1978; New York, 1979). *Sam Shepard: Seven Plays.* New York: Bantam, 1981.

Seduced (New York, 1978). *Fool for Love and Other Plays.* New York: Bantam, 1984.

Shaved Splits (New York, 1970). *The Unseen Hand and Other Plays.* Indianapolis: Bobbs-Merrill, 1972.

Suicide in B^b (New Haven, 1976; New York, 1984). *Fool for Love and Other Plays.* New York: Bantam, 1984.

BIBLIOGRAPHY

Tongues (San Francisco, 1978; New York, 1979) *Sam Shepard: Seven Plays*. New York: Bantam, 1981.

The Tooth of Crime (London, 1972; New York, 1973). *Sam Shepard: Seven Plays*. New York: Bantam, 1981.

True West (San Francisco, 1980; New York, 1980). *Sam Shepard: Seven Plays*. New York: Bantam, 1981.

The Unseen Hand (New York, 1969). *The Unseen Hand and Other Plays*. Indianapolis: Bobbs-Merrill, 1972.

Up to Thursday (New York, 1965). Manuscript.

Primary Sources: Screenplays

Me and My Brother (1967).

Zabriskie Point (1970). Co-author with Michaelangelo Antonioni, Antonino Guerra, and others.

Ringaleevio (1971).

Paris, Texas (1984).

Fool for Love (1985).

Secondary Sources

Auerbach, Doris. *Sam Shepard, Arthur Kopit and the Off Broadway Theater*. Boston: Twayne, 1982. More than a third of the book is devoted to an analytic survey of Shepard's plays. The emphasis is on his literary connections.

Blau, Herbert. "The American Dream Set in American Gothic: The Plays of Sam Shepard and Adrienne Kennedy." *Modern Drama* 27.4 (1984): 520–39. Asserts that although the concept of the American Dream has been overly studied by American scholarship, it is no less alluring, and in the plays of Shepard and Kennedy is found a Gothicized, nightmarish, up-to-date variant on its major premises. Discusses *Tooth of Crime, Curse of the Starving Class, Buried Child* by Shepard and *Funnyhouse of a Negro, A Rat's Mass, A Movie Star Has to Star in Black and White*, and *The Owl Answers* by Kennedy.

BIBLIOGRAPHY

Chubb, Kenneth, et al, eds. "Metaphors, Mad Dogs and Old Time Cowboys: Interview with Sam Shepard." *American Dreams: The Imagination of Sam Shepard*, Ed. Bonnie Marranca. New York: Performing Arts Journal Publications, 1981. 187–209. A long and important interview with Shepard on his life, career, and esthetics, focusing especially on *The Tooth of Crime* and *Geography of a Horse Dreamer*.

Gilman, Richard. Introduction. *Sam Shepard: Seven Plays*. New York: Bantam, 1984. Offers insights into Shepard's life, times, and work, especially the plays collected here.

Kleb, William. "Worse than Being Homeless: *True West* and the Divided Self." *American Dreams: The Imagination of Sam Shepard*. Ed. Bonnie Marranca. New York: Peforming Arts Journal Publications, 1981. 117–25. Discusses the play in "territorial" terms as well as in terms of the mythic West and Shepard's relations to it.

Kroll, Jack. "Who's That Tall, Dark Stranger?" *Newsweek* 11 Nov. 1985: 68–74. An up-to-date biographical essay, focusing on Shepard's status as a public figure.

Levy, Jacques. "Notes on *Red Cross*." *Chicago and Other Plays*. By Sam Shepard. New York: Urizen, 1981. 96–98. The director of *Red Cross* generalizes shrewdly about the nature of Shepard's art.

Marranca, Bonnie, ed. *American Dreams: The Imagination of Sam Shepard*. New York: Performing Arts Journal Publications, 1981. An important source book for the student of Shepard. Contains 24 contributions from critics, actors, directors, friends, and Shepard himself.

Mottram, Ron. *Inner Landscapes: The Theater of Sam Shepard*. Columbia: University of Missouri Press, 1984. The first full-length critical work on Shepard; gives consistently ac-

BIBLIOGRAPHY

curate analyses of all the work up to but not including *A Lie of the Mind.*

Nash, Thomas. "Sam Shepard's's *Buried Child*: The Ironic Use of Folklore." *Modern Drama* 24 (1983): 486–91. Argues convincingly for Shepard's use of the corn-king ritual of death and rebirth.

Orbison, Tucker. "Mythic Levels in Shepard's *True West.*" *Modern Drama* 27 (1984): 506–19. An analysis of the mysterious, spiritual elements in the play: the split psyche, the mystery of the artist, the primacy of consciousness. On the split psyche, it develops a convincing parallel between the characters in the play and the American character described by D. H. Lawrence in *Studies in Classic American Literature.*

Shepard, Sam. "Language, Visualization and the Inner Library." *American Dreams: The Imagination of Sam Shepard.* Ed. Bonnie Marranca. New York: Performing Arts Journal Publications, 1981. 214–19. A very valuable and articulate statement by Shepard on the inner workings of the artist's mind and soul.

Smith, Michael. Notes on *Icarus's Mother. Chicago and Other Plays.* By Sam Shepard. New York: Urizen, 1981. 26–29. Another director of Shepard's work speaks with insight about the playwright's art.

Lanford Wilson

Primary Sources: Plays

Angels Fall (Miami, 1982; New York, 1982). New York: Hill and Wang, 1983.

Balm in Gilead (New York, 1965). *Balm in Gilead and Other Plays.* New York: Hill and Wang, 1965.

BIBLIOGRAPHY

Brontosaurus (New York, 1977). New York: Dramatists Play
   Service, 1978.

Common Thyme (New York, 1981). Manuscript.

Days Ahead (New York, 1965). *The Rimers of Eldritch and Other
   Plays*. New York: Hill and Wang, 1967.

The Family Continues (New York, 1972). *The Great Nebula in
   Orion and Three Other Plays*. New York: Dramatists Play
   Service, 1973.

5th of July (New York, 1978, 1980). New York: Dramatists
   Play Service, 1982. *The Best Plays of 1977–79*. Ed. Otis
   Guernsey. New York: Dodd, Mead, 1979.

The Gingham Dog (Washington, 1968; New York, 1969). New
   York: Hill and Wang, 1970.

The Great Nebula in Orion. (Manchester, England, 1970; New
   York, 1972). *The Great Nebula in Orion and Three Other
   Plays*. New York: Dramatists Play Service, 1973.

Home Free! (New York, 1964) *Balm in Gilead and Other Plays.*
   New York: Hill and Wang, 1965. *The Madness of Lady
   Bright and Home Free!* London: Methuen, 1968.

Hot l Baltimore (New York, 1973). New York: Hill and Wang,
   1973; New York: Dramatists Play Service, 1973.

Ikke, Ikke, Nye, Nye, Nye (New York, 1972). *The Great Nebula
   in Orion and Three Other Plays*. New York: Dramatists Play
   Service, 1973.

Lemon Sky (Waterford, CT, 1968; New York, 1970). New
   York: Hill and Wang, 1970; New York: Dramatists Play
   Service, 1971. *Best American Plays, 7th Series: 1967–1973*,
   ed. Clive Barnes and John Gassner. New York: Crown,
   1975.

Ludlow Fair (New York, 1965). *Balm in Gilead and Other Plays.*
   New York: Hill and Wang, 1965.

The Madness of Lady Bright (New York, 1966). *The Madness of*

BIBLIOGRAPHY

Lady Bright and Home Free! London: Methuen, 1968. New York: Dramatists Play Service, 1970.

Miss Williams: A Turn (New York, 1967). Manuscript.

The Mound Builders (New York, 1975). New York: Hill and Wang, 1976.

No Trespassing (New York, 1964). Manuscript.

The Rimers of Eldritch (New York 1967). *The Rimers of Eldritch and Other Plays.* New York: Hill and Wang, 1967. New York: Dramatists Play Service, 1967.

The Sand Castle (New York, 1965). *The Sand Castle and Three Other Plays.* New York: Dramatists Play Service, 1970.

Serenading Louie (Washington, 1970; New York, 1976). New York: Dramatists Play Service, 1977.

Sex Is Between Two People (New York, 1965). Manuscript.

Sextet (Yes): A Play for Voices (New York, 1971). *The Sand Castle and Three Other Plays.* New York: Dramatists Play Service, 1970.

So Long at the Fair (New York, 1963). Manuscript.

Stoop (New York, 1970). *The Sand Castle and Three Other Plays.* New York: Dramatists Play Service, 1970.

Summer and Smoke (1971). Opera libretto. Manuscript.

A Tale Told (New York, 1981). Manuscript. Revised as *Talley & Son.*

Talley & Son (Saratoga Springs, 1985; New York, 1985). Manuscript. Publication due in 1987.

Talley's Folly (New York, 1979). New York: Hill and Wang, 1980.

This Is the Rill Speaking (New York, 1965). *The Rimers of Eldritch and Other Plays.* New York: Hill and Wang, 1967.

Untitled Play (Music by Al Carmines; New York, 1967). Manuscript.

Victory on Mrs. Dandywine's Island (1970). *The Great Nebula in*

BIBLIOGRAPHY

Orion & Three Other Plays. New York: Dramatists Play Service, 1973.

Wandering: A Turn (New York, 1966). *The Rimers of Eldritch and Other Plays*. New York: Hill and Wang, 1967. *The Sand Castle and Three Other Plays*. New York: Dramatists Play Service, 1970.

Secondary Sources

Cohn, Ruby. "Broadway Bound: Simon, Kopit, McNally, Wilson." *New American Dramatists: 1960–1980*. New York: Grove, 1982. 8–26. A highly compressed but accurate survey of Wilson's major work and tendencies.

Marranca, Bonnie, and Gautam Dasgupta. *American Playwrights: A Critical Survey*. New York: Drama Book Specialists, 1981. Contains a very detailed survey of Wilson's whole oeuvre. Touches on themes of loss, nostalgia, America, and describes the technique of poetic realism.

Paul, John Steven., "'Who Are You? Who are We?': Two Questions Raised in Lanford Wilson's *Talley's Folly*." Valparaiso *Cresset* Sept. 1980: 25–27. Links the play to a central tradition of American drama, plays that place the identity of the characters above plot development or genre.

Schvey, Henry I. "Images of the Past in the Plays of Lanford Wilson." *Essays in Contemporary American Drama*. Ed. Hedwig Bock and Albert Wertheim. Munich: Hueber, 1981. 225–40. Using the major works from *Hot 1 Baltimore* through *Talley's Folly*, discusses how the plays lament for things once beautiful but now lost.

Witham, Barry. "Images of America: Wilson, Weller, Horovitz." *Theatre Journal* 34 (1982):223–32. Considering works that use the quintessential July image, Witham analyses *5th of July*. Explains that although Wilson sees

BIBLIOGRAPHY

much of America as a failed promise, he also dramatizes America as a garden where there is hope of renewal.

General Works

Auerbach, Doris. *Sam Shepard, Arthur Kopit and the Off Broadway Theatre.* Boston: Twayne, 1982. Good on both playwrights and interesting on aspects of the Off Broadway theater.

Berkowitz, Gerald M. *New Broadways: Theatre Across America 1950–1980.* Totowa, NJ: Littlefield, 1982. Provides a detailed history of the founding and development of theaters outside the mainstream of Broadway.

Bigsby, C. W. E. *A Critical Introduction to Twentieth-Century American Drama*, vol. 3. New York: Cambridge University Press, 1985. The definitive work on the period. Treats many playwrights separately, with full chapters on Mamet and Shepard.

Cohn, Ruby. *New American Dramatists: 1960–1980.* New York: Grove, 1982. Condensed but accurate surveys of thirty American playwrights and the contexts of their work.

Little, Stuart W. *Off Broadway: The Prophetic Theatre.* New York: Coward, McCann, 1972. A detailed history of the people, the plays, and the circumstances.

Marranca, Bonnie, and Gautam Dasgupta. *American Playwrights: A Critical Survey.* New York: Drama Book Specialists, 1981. Good surveys of eighteen playwrights who were produced before 1967 in major Off Broadway theaters; by the editors of *Performing Arts Journal.*

Shank, Theodore. *American Alternative Theatre.* New York: Oxford University Press, 1982. Good on modern American avant-garde.